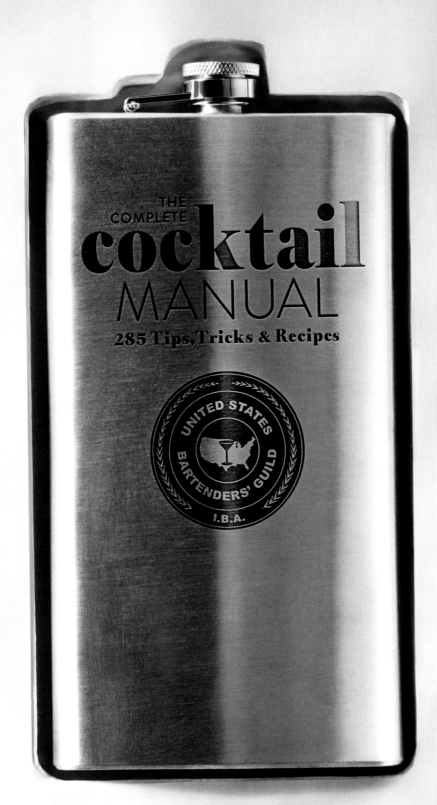

THE
COMPLETE
cocktail
MANUAL

285 Tips, Tricks & Recipes

UNITED STATES
BARTENDERS' GUILD
I.B.A.

THE
COMPLETE
cocktail
MANUAL

285 Tips, Tricks & Recipes

LOU BUSTAMANTE

weldon**owen**

ENTERTAINING & HOSPITALITY

ABOUT THE USBG

The United States Bartenders' Guild (USBG) is a trade organization dedicated to supporting and strengthening the professional development of bartenders throughout the country. With chapters in over 70 cities and more than 6,000 members, the USBG develops innovative opportunities for bartenders to accelerate their professional pursuits.

With the increased interest in both the craft and profession, the USBG fills a vital role in helping shape the future of the beverage and hospitality industries through collaboration with an interactive network of professional bartenders, educational events, and community service projects. In other words, they help make your drinks and experience better when you go to a bar.

The USBG is the only domestic organization represented in the International Bartenders Association (IBA). With this global partnership, the USBG connects American beverage professionals with peers around the world. Members can develop key industry contacts—from international camaraderie to local chapter connections.

The organization allows less experienced members to grow, and more experienced members to mentor—and together elevate not only the quality of the cocktail, but also the profession as a whole. It is this insight and passion that we hope will make you a better bartender at home.

THE COCKTAIL HAS CHANGED

In the last decade or two, the bar world has seen an evolution—there is now more interest in the craft of mixing drinks as well as increased scrutiny of the ingredients that go into them. Local, artisanal, and unique: it isn't just for food anymore.

Just as chefs are concerned about the ingredients they cook with, bartenders are increasingly examining the brands of spirits they stock and mix with. Marketing-driven brand preference by customers has long dominated, but destination bars are starting to do away with poorly made, mass-market liquors, favoring instead those spirits that are made skillfully and responsibly.

This doesn't mean that all large brands are poor in quality, nor that all small ones are good. Many of the best liquors to mix with come from big companies, but stocking interesting spirits and introducing customers to unique brands can define a bar's personality and add value to the experience.

There is also a movement to simplify. The best bartenders are not over-innovating, instead using off-the-shelf ingredients combined with select homemade items to customize their drinks.

But what's most remarkable about the recent cocktail revolution is that it is merely one aspect of the overall bar experience. The atmosphere of today's bars—lighting, furniture, and layout—is important, but service is paramount. Having a great drink is crucial, but having a wonderful time even more so.

The preciousness and conceit that plagued the arm-garter years has been replaced with a desire to get you what you want and get it to you quickly, in a comfortable and enjoyable way. The art of hospitality is back.

To help guide you through the modern era of bartending, and welcome you to the modern art of mixing and serving cocktails is the collective wisdom of the United States Bartenders' Guild (USBG), a trade organization of over 70 chapters across the United States and a part of the International Bartenders Association (IBA).

From setting up your bar, building a menu, and hosting the year's best cocktail party, this book has you covered.

Cheers,

Lou Bustamante
San Francisco Chapter

Basics & Setup

We get it, you're thirsty. You probably want to skip ahead to the second chapter so you can start mixing drinks instead of reading about supplies and equipment, the processes by which liquor is made, and all the other things you need to know to properly set up your home bar. Well, if that's what you want to do, go for it. We'll be here waiting when you can't figure out how to store your growing collection of bottles, how long all that stuff keeps, and which supplies you really need to spend your money on.

Oh, back already? Good, because there's a lot to learn—but don't worry, nothing about the art of barkeeping is boring. So, cozy up to your local bar with an old favorite (or grab that drink you learned to make in chapter two if you decided to read ahead) and let's teach you some basics.

Sure, fundamentals might not be as sexy as a perfectly made Manhattan—but they will help you make sure that it is perfect, every time.

001 CHOOSE YOUR DRINK

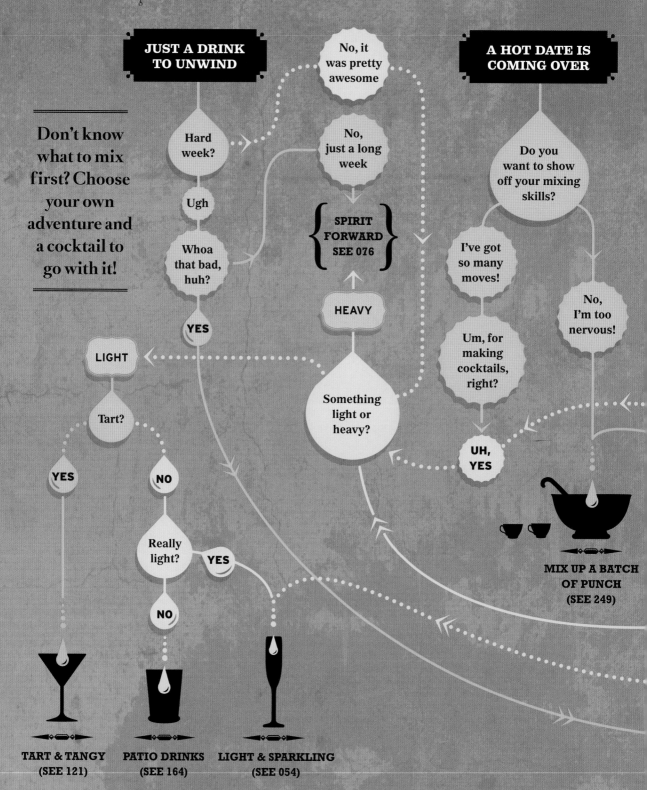

Don't know what to mix first? Choose your own adventure and a cocktail to go with it!

JUST A DRINK TO UNWIND

A HOT DATE IS COMING OVER

No, it was pretty awesome

No, just a long week

Hard week?

Ugh

Whoa that bad, huh?

YES

LIGHT

Tart?

YES

NO

Really light?

YES

NO

SPIRIT FORWARD SEE 076

HEAVY

Something light or heavy?

Do you want to show off your mixing skills?

I've got so many moves!

Um, for making cocktails, right?

No, I'm too nervous!

UH, YES

MIX UP A BATCH OF PUNCH (SEE 249)

TART & TANGY (SEE 121)

PATIO DRINKS (SEE 164)

LIGHT & SPARKLING (SEE 054)

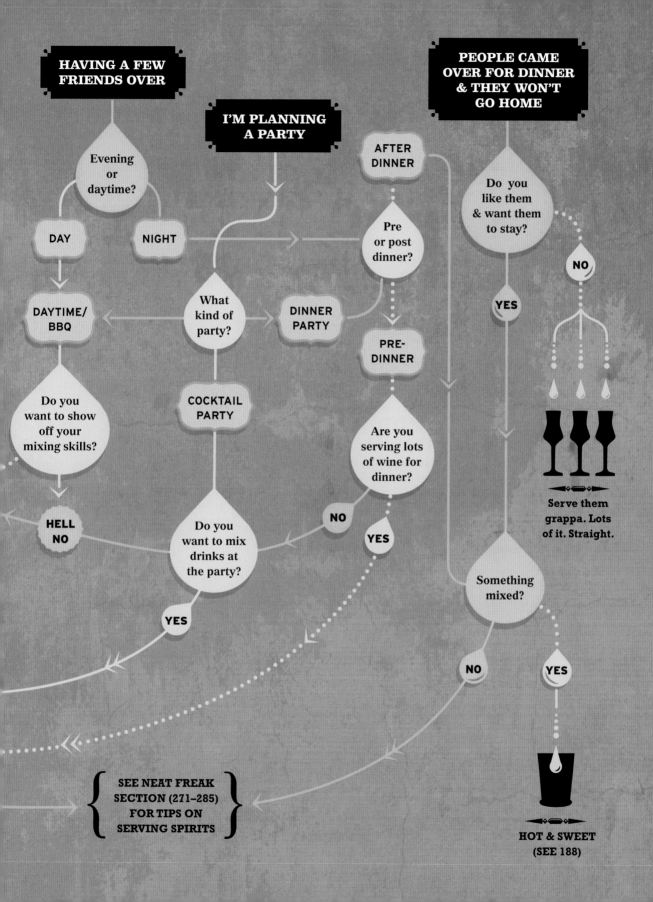

002 | SHAKING & POURING

SHAKE IT TILL YOU MAKE IT

Learning to make cocktails at home is a lot less challenging than it may seem. Invest in a few key pieces of equipment and supplies, and the rewards will be well worth the effort. After a long day or a sudden warm spell of weather, a cocktail at home is incredibly satisfying. Here's where to get started.

LEARN AT YOUR LOCAL BAR If you have no idea what kinds of drinks you like, start your education by visiting your favorite local bar on a quiet day and consulting with your bartender. Talk about the flavors you enjoy and let him or her guide you to new drinks. You can also consult our drink flowchart (see item 001) and give it a whirl to find a match.

ACCEPT ACQUIRED TASTES We all have different preferences for levels of sweet, tart, bitter, and potency. Feel free to adjust as needed to suit your tastes, but don't be afraid to try new things, either—you might be surprised at how your palate can evolve.

003 { PRACTICE, PRACTICE, PRACTICE }

Like any skill, learning the art of making cocktails and mixing a proper drink takes work—and lots of practice. Here are a few things to keep in mind as you shake and stir your way through this book.

FIND A PRACTICE SPACE Before you invest in a bar or cart (and any expensive bottles), carve out a little space on a countertop where you can mix and experiment. You can also store your equipment and bottles here for easy access. Make sure the countertop is at a comfortable height for standing.

START OVER Sometimes a drink just doesn't work out. Sometimes you might accidentally pour too much of something, or you lose track of where you were and leave something out. Whatever the reason, don't be afraid to dump it out and start all over. The extra effort will be worth it.

MAKE ADJUSTMENTS Even within the same category, spirits can vary in flavor—and it will sometimes impact the cocktail's balance. Varying levels of sweetness in liqueurs, oak flavor in aged spirits, and the botanicals in gin can shift a drink off balance even with the simplest of recipes. Don't be afraid to throw the drink back in the mixing glass or shaker and add more sweetness or acidity.

BEGIN WITH THE BASICS The easiest way to get creative with your drinks is to start with a recipe you already like and go from there, rather than wildly mixing random ingredients together. Learn how to make an old favorite, first, and then try swapping out an ingredient or two, or substituting a few different elements. You'll be surprised how different the variations can taste.

004

SPEAK IN TONGUES

Cocktail terminology may be obvious to some, but I've overheard enough misused terms from the next barstool to know we might as well include a reminder for those—not you, of course—who may need it.

BACK A chaser, usually a short pour of soda, beer, or other liquid (like pickle juice)—or even some kind of snack. The back either complements the flavors of whatever is being chased or washes away the taste (not a good sign).

CALL To ask for. When you order a drink and ask for a particular spirit, you call for it.

DRY Low in sweetness, often used to order a martini with very little vermouth.

LONG A drink served in a tall glass. You can sometimes request drinks that come with soda mixers to be served long with extra mixer.

NEAT Liquor served in a glass without ice and at room temperature, usually when you are enjoying a nice, expensive spirit. Differs from a shot in that it is served in a short (old-fashioned or rocks) glass and meant to be sipped.

(ON THE) ROCKS A drink served in a short glass with ice. Rocks are ice cubes.

TWIST The peel of a citrus fruit, often twisted near the drink to express the fragrant oils before being dropped in.

UP A drink served in a coupe or cocktail glass with no ice but always chilled.

WELL LIQUOR The house brands of liquor used to make a majority of the drinks. Asking for something that sits on the backbar (not in the well) is often a premium call (and costs more money).

005 | BUILD YOUR TOOL KIT

↦ MUDDLER OR HAND JUICER A good muddler is essential for incorporating bold flavors from fresh herbs and fruits into a cocktail. Fresh juice is critical in a good cocktail, and the best juicing tool when making drinks on a small scale is a citrus press. They're fast, extract both fragrant citrus oils (from the peels and rinds) and juices, and they clean up easily.

↦ CORKSCREW AND BOTTLE OPENER The waiter's corkscrew, with a lever and a bottle opener, is all you'll need to open any kind of bottle.

↦ STRAINER There are two basic types of strainers: a Hawthorne (which has a loose spring forming a half circle on the lip), and a julep (which looks like a squat, slotted spoon), but you probably only need the Hawthorne—the julep is for stirred drinks, but often a Hawthorne fits and works better.

↦ TONGS When handling ice, stainless-steel tongs are a must to keep the temperature down. They can also come in handy when grabbing garnishes.

JIGGER Free-pouring (mixing without using measuring tools) is a skill that takes time to develop; until then, please measure—a fraction of an ounce can turn a great drink into a bad one. Double-ended jiggers are great for speed but not for flexibility—if you need a quarter ounce of something, you'll have to eyeball it. The small measuring-cup-style ones are a better choice for beginners.

cocktails. The variations in style are endless, but st[...] to two-part shakers, such as French or Boston styl[...] Three-part shakers, where the strainer is built int[...] top, can freeze up at the seams (see item 116).

BAR SPOON Use a bar spoon for making stirred drinks and fishing cherries out of their jars. You can also use a long spoon, like those for iced tea; but if you don't have one, it's easy to find a nice, inexpensive bar spoon.

006

DISTILL YOUR BEER, WINE, OR SMOOTHIE

➤➤ The first step for making all types of distilled spirits starts with a fermented liquid of some kind, typically a wine or beer, but not the kind of finished drink you usually enjoy in a glass on its own. Thin, acidic, and often bland, the importance of the ferment goes beyond its alcoholic content—it provides flavor foundation and even defines what it can be called.

GRAIN Corn, wheat, rye, rice, barley, and other grains get fermented into a mash or beer and become the backbone of whiskies (with barrel aging), and other spirits like vodka and gin. A portion of the grain in the mashbill (recipe) must be malted, a process in which the grain is allowed to germinate and promote the release of enzymes, like amylase, that convert starches to sugars. Alternatively, the enzyme must be added directly. The new fermented liquid smells and looks a lot like malty, unfiltered beer—but without the hops it tastes oddly thin and watery.

VEGETABLE OR MINERAL

Admittedly, "mineral" might be a stretch—you can't ferment rocks—but anything with accessible sugars for yeast to feed on can become the base for a distilled spirit. Vegetables, particularly sugar beets and potatoes, are common for vodka or as a base for other spirits— although they are usually distilled for the alcohol alone. Plants like agave are crucial for making tequila and mezcal. Sugarcane and molasses are the bases for all rum, while sorghum (another grass) is used in Chinese *baiju*, a potent liquor. We've also tasted distilled spirits made from milk, sweet potatoes, carrots, and even maple syrup—all quite good.

FRUIT Fermenting fruit will produce a type of wine; once distilled, it becomes brandy. Typical spirits made from fruit are Cognac (grapes), Armagnac (also grapes), Calvados (apples), grappa/marc (leftover solids from winemaking), Pisco (grapes), slivovitz (plums), kirsch (cherries), Poire Williams (pears), and eau-de-vie (an extremely aromatic style of brandy that showcases one particular fruit like apricots, raspberries, or peaches). Keep in mind that these brandies are not flavored with the fruit but are actually made from it.

007 | RUN YOUR STILL WATERS DEEP (AND TALL)

The gleaming copper and stainless-steel machines outfitted with precision instrumentation can make distillation seem complex. But at its core, the process is nothing more than boiling a liquid. By gently heating the ferment, the lighter alcohol and aromatic compounds attached to alcohol (with a boiling point of 172°F/78°C) evaporate up the still before the water does (at 212°F/100°C) and collect in the condenser. There are a few basic styles of stills used in distillation.

ALEMBIC The alembic is the oldest style of still; it originated in the 9th century and evolved into the ornate and essential stills of Cognac and other brandy producers. The bulbous cap and swan's neck create surface areas for condensation that force water and impurities to stay behind.

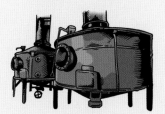

POT The alembic is technically a type of pot still, but not all pot stills are alembics. In its simplest form, a pot still is a pot over a heat source with a cap of some kind and a tube to extract the distillate. Pot stills are inefficient but can allow more flavor and nuance to show up in the final product.

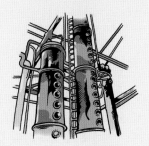

COLUMN A column still is a large metal tube filled with plates and valves that create obstructions for the alcohol and water vapors to condense. Columns are usually used in situations where fewer impurities (less flavor) and higher proof are needed, such as in the production of vodka. A single column or an array can be attached to a pot still.

CONTINUOUS A continuous still is an array of column stills—typically multistory affairs that are magnificently efficient at making high-proof alcohol and commodity-grade spirits. While a pot still needs to be filled, run, and emptied with each run, continuous stills—as the name implies—have a constant stream of ferment going in, condensing and vaporizing through the columns, and being collected at precise proofs.

008 { SIP THE BASICS OF BARREL AGING }

Barrel aging has been around since the time of the Roman Empire, as has the preference for oak casks. The process of aging, while slow, can completely transform a brash and unruly alcoholic beverage. Here's a look at what makes a good barrel.

TYPE Two types of oak are typically used: French and American. American oak is high in lactones (think coconut and peach) and lignin (vanilla), and the intensity of the flavors is enhanced by the kiln drying process. French oak tends to have less tannin than American oak, due in part to the French custom of seasoning the wood outdoors for several years before constructing the barrels. Tannin, while bitter, provides richness in flavor. Hemicellulose, which imparts a toasty quality, is found in both types of oak and, along with lignin, will break down over time into sugars, masking the harshness of the alcohol.

TOAST Toasting a barrel over an open fire can drastically change the flavor of the liquor, due to the caramelization of wood sugars, the concentration of vanillin, the roasted flavors (furanic aldehydes), and the smoky and spice notes (eugenol). Barrels can also be toasted to an intense char that results in charcoal forming inside the barrel, which has the benefit of absorbing smelly sulphur-based compounds.

PROOF The alcohol content by volume (ABV) of the liquid being aged in a barrel plays an important role in how it ages. Oak compounds are more soluble in alcohol than water, so a whiskey will draw out more wood flavor than a wine will. More important, the ABV will change as the cask ages since the semiporous environment allows water and alcohol to evaporate out.

OXIDATION The watertight yet breathable nature of wood allows for evaporation out, but it also allows oxygen to get in. In wine, this exposure to oxygen helps maintain the color, but it also reacts with alcohol and oil from the oak to develop aromas in both wine and spirits.

REUSE There are plenty of situations in which a new barrel isn't needed, such as when the presence of the oak flavors need to be tamed. When the flavors from the distillate need to be showcased—such as in tequila, scotch, and some brandies—the spirits often end up in used barrels, and they still get the benefits of oxidation and some oak flavors.

009

GET OVER THE BARREL

While barrel aging can enhance flavor, there's a limit to its power—and there are quite a few things that can go wrong. If you're dropping big bucks on something aged more than 20 years, try it at a bar first—and don't believe everything you're told.

→ OLDER ISN'T BETTER The default theory is that the older the spirit, the better (and more expensive) it will be. While this can be true, it isn't always the case. Overaged spirits have overextracted compounds from the wood, like tannin, which can make it bitter and overwhelm it with a lumberyard's worth of wood in aroma and taste.

→ AGE DOESN'T MEAN FLAVOR There are some aromas and flavors—a certain brightness and freshness—that can get lost after too much time in the barrel. Brandies, tequila, and even wines can wither from too much time in oak, like a wood-flavored mute button suppressing the fruit.

→ BARREL AGE CAN LIE The climate where the barrels age impact how much extraction of oak ends up in the final product. A barrel aged in a cold location will age slower than one in the tropics—warmth speeds up the aging process, while cold slows it down. So a Scottish whisky can age for a longer amount of time than a Jamaican rum can.

→ SPIRITS DON'T AGE IN THE BOTTLE Sorry to break it to you, but that special 20-year-old Scotch that's been sitting in your cabinet for the last five years is not a 25-year-old bottle. Age only happens in barrels—and bad things can happen to a bottle if it's not properly stored (see item 010).

010

KEEP IT UNDER COVER

Properly storing your spirits will not only ensure that your drinks taste good but also that those expensive bottles of liquor you bought to treat yourself don't wind up down the drain. For the most part, standard spirits like vodka, tequila, mezcal, gin, and all the whiskies should keep indefinitely. Liqueurs that are herbal or citrusy, such as triple sec, should keep for a very long time as well. Just follow these easy rules.

STORE BOTTLES UPRIGHT Your wine bottles may be fine lying on their sides in a rack, but spirits, with their much-higher alcohol content, don't do as well on their sides. If the bottle uses a natural cork top, chances are good that storage in this position will eat away at the cork, leaving sediment inside or leaking liquid out.

KEEP AWAY FROM HEAT AND LIGHT Sunlight and heat will destroy your booze by creating sediment and changing the color and flavor. It might make things taste funky or even lose any flavor completely, making it tasteless. If you want to show off a collection, make sure to store only empty bottles by the window.

KEEP THE BOTTLES SEALED Don't lose each bottle's cap or top—and if you do, either finish or dump the bottle. You need to maintain a good seal to maintain a good spirit.

USE YOUR SENSES If you're not sure if your liquor has spoiled, the best thing to do is closely examine the bottle. If it looks or smells funky, or if something seems off, it probably is. If you still aren't sure, taste it—most high-proof spirits don't biologically spoil, so a small sip of a bad spirit won't harm you—aside from leaving a bad taste in your mouth.

011

BUY SIZE SMART

When buying aromatized wines, like vermouth, to use in cocktails, look for the increasingly popular smaller-size bottles. They're easy to find at most retailers, and a 375 ml bottle is usually all you'll need—it boasts enough to make 12 standard Manhattans or 24 gin martinis. Remember that vermouth will only keep for two months—and, as with any wine, fresher is always better.

012 ❖ CLEAN YOUR BAR

Even a beginner likely has a few bottles and ingredients lying around the house–but we recommend doing a little purging to get rid of those that may do more harm than good. If you don't remember when you opened it, it's best to toss it.

PRODUCT	REFRIGERATE?	SHELF LIFE (OPENED)
Cream liqueur	Yes	12 months; 3 weeks if homemade
Fruit liqueur (made with fruit, not flavored)	Yes	Varies with the amount and type of juice
Vermouth	Yes	2 months, although the fresher the better
Cocktail syrup	Yes	2 months
Simple syrup	Yes	3-4 weeks
Grenadine	Yes	3 months
Lime cordial	No	3 months
Cocktail cherries	Yes	6 months
Martini olives	Yes	12 months
Juice (canned and fresh)	Yes	Varies by fruit and oxidation; 2-5 days
Bitters	No	As long as it takes to empty the bottle

013 | BUILD YOUR BACKBAR

➤➤ Choosing what bottles to buy when you first start mixing cocktails can be a little overwhelming. Liquor store shelves are filled with hundreds of bottles per type of spirit, and the simple act of choosing one bottle can be intimidating (and not just for the newbie).

If you can, skip the discount retail store in favor of a place with knowledgeable staff and good service. At nicer shops, the staff will be up to date on the stock they carry and often taste most of what they sell, meaning they can guide you toward bottles that fit your needs.

Don't start with the expensive picks; find the midrange bottles that offer quality and will work well in mixed drinks. For white spirits like vodka and gin, you can find good-quality bottles in the $20–$30 USD range.

Start slow, and grow your bar organically by choosing one cocktail you like and buying supplies for just that drink. Then choose another recipe and go from there—pretty soon you'll have a collection that works best for your tastes.

014 { ASSEMBLE VERSATILE BOTTLES }

To give you a sense of what a versatile collection of bottles for bartending looks like, USBG bartender Kevin Diedrich (San Francisco Chapter) of PCH (Pacific Cocktail Haven) compiled his ideal ingredient lists—for both beginners and more advanced barkeep —that will allow you to make the most of the drinks in this book.

BEGINNER

○ Vodka

○ Gin

○ Rum

○ Tequila

○ Bourbon

○ Rye

○ Blended Scotch

○ Small Sweet Vermouth

○ Small Dry Vermouth

○ Angostura Bitters

○ Peychaud's Bitters

○ Orange Bitters

○ Triple Sec

○ Maraschino liqueur

○ Benedictine liqueur

INTERMEDIATE/ ADVANCED

Same as Beginner but adding

○ Mezcal

○ Green Chartreuse

○ Lillet Blanc

○ Absinthe

○ Cognac

○ Dark Rum

○ Light Rum

○ Campari

015 { SHERRY UP, GET THE VERMOUTH OUT }

Sherry and vermouth are fortified wines, meaning that distilled spirits have been added to them to arrest fermentation. They are often consumed alone but can also be mixed into drinks like martinis or negronis.

SHERRY Traditionally, sherry is made in Spain and comes in a range of styles that runs the gamut of dry fino or Manzanilla to sweet cream and Pedro Ximénez. Some sherry is aged under a raft of yeast that covers the exposed sherry and protects it from contact with oxygen, but others are purposefully oxidized. Manzanilla Pasada, amontillado, palo cortado, and oloroso are among those purposefully exposed to oxygen; the oxidation process adds richness and nut flavors.

Although sherries are fortified, the more delicate ones will suffer from oxidation, so treat them like you would any wine and try to enjoy them immediately after opening. Some oxidized varieties like amontillado can keep for much longer, although their flavor will change over time.

VERMOUTH The name for vermouth actually comes from the German *wermut*, or "wormwood," which is the chief botanical that defines vermouth. Despite the hysteria that revolved around the hallucinogenic properties of wormwood in absinthe, no one ever complained about seeing green fairies from drinking vermouth. Nevertheless, the use and amount of wormwood was decreased in many brands.

Vermouth comes in a variety of styles: dry (or French), white (a sweet version of dry), red (or sweet, or Italian), and rosé. The flavors vary greatly, even among similar styles, because each producer has his or her own botanical recipe—like most wines. Pick up a few small bottles and keep testing until you find what works best for you.

016

STOCK YOUR CELLAR

↬ Stocking your bar with bottles isn't just about hard liquor; it's also about beer and wine. Aside from mixing an occasional sangria (see item 177), *michelada* (see item 182), or shandy (see item 180), you'll probably be serving your beer and wine as is, so the type you select should suit the event. A party where most people are standing is probably not the right event for fancy wine served in delicate glassware. Instead, look for drinks that balance value and quality, and also note what kind of food will be served. Remember, cheese works with pretty much everything. Whatever you choose, do a little research on the winery or brewery in case anyone is curious— putting thought into even the inexpensive wines is always impressive. This doesn't work, however, if you serve supermarket brands—no one is going to need to ask you anything if you serve Natty Ice—except "*Seriously?*"

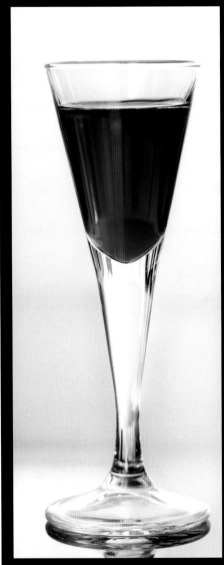

017

IMBIBE SWEET LIQUOR

Liqueurs are one of the oldest types of distilled spirit beverages, and they're nothing more than sweetened liquor. At first, liqueurs were the specialty of monks—they used alcohol as a medium to create medicinal herb tonics, and added sweeteners to make them more palatable.

Technically speaking, in order for something to be called a liqueur, it must have at least 2.5 percent sweetener by weight—flavored by distillation, infusion, or extracts. Another class of liqueurs called crèmes must contain at least 25 percent sugar, and while usually dairy-free, their name comes from the syrupy, creamy texture of the liqueur (thanks to large amounts of sugar).

018 { WATCH YOUR SUGAR CONTENT }

The thing to keep in mind about liqueurs is that the sweetness levels can vary significantly, and the percentage (which could range from 2.5 to 25 percent) is not listed on the bottle. This means that you should always taste a cocktail when swapping out brands or trying a new type of liqueur in a recipe. Try it out on a half-size recipe first—and remember that cold liquids taste less sweet than those at room temperature, so make sure your test includes the shaking or stirring process, too.

019

FIND YOUR SWEET SPOT

The sheer number of flavors liqueurs come in can be baffling, and while you'll never need more than a couple of bottles for your home bar, it's always good to know what's out there.

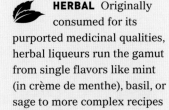 **HERBAL** Originally consumed for its purported medicinal qualities, herbal liqueurs run the gamut from single flavors like mint (in crème de menthe), basil, or sage to more complex recipes like the Carthusian monk specialty chartreuse.

BITTER This style of liqueurs can be served both predinner (aperitif) and postdinner (digestif), and their recipes can contain every plant from a botanical garden and anything traded on the spice road. The bitterness comes from traditional ingredients like cinchona bark and gentian root, but it can also be added with hops or a high concentration of citrus peels.

FRUIT The biggest category involves almost every fruit imaginable: raspberries, apricots, peaches, bananas, you name it. These also tend to be the most susceptible to oxidation, so buy small bottles, or plan on drinking the liqueurs while they're fresh.

CITRUS The most common in mixed drinks, citrus-based liqueurs like triple sec and curaçao give drinks a brightness you can't get from juice alone. Citrus is the only style you need to have in your basic home bar.

SLOE GIN This gin-based liqueur gets flavored with tart sloe berries that meld nicely with the juniper and other botanicals.

 CREAM These dairy liqueurs add richness to drinks and are fridge stable for a very long time, making them terrifying in their longevity—and deliciousness.

 COFFEE Jolts of caffeine and coffee flavor make these liqueurs a great alternative to hot coffee at the end of a meal.

CHOCOLATE You'll mostly find chocolate presented via crème de cacao, but more chocolate liqueurs are popping up from artisanal producers. They're a great way to add rich chocolate flavor.

SPICE The spice rack in liquid form allows you to think with a culinary mind when mixing up cocktails. You've probably already had zesty ginger, so why not try saffron, allspice, or anise?

NUTS Great for both baking and mixing, nut liqueurs are the most popular in almond, hazelnut, and walnut flavors.

FLORAL Flower liqueurs are like drinkable perfumes, and, as with fragrant foods, too much in a cocktail can make them taste soapy. You'll find the ever-popular elderflower on the shelf alongside a whole garden's worth, including violet, hibiscus, poppy, and rose.

020 | BOAST BETTER BITTERS

Historically speaking, cocktails by definition had bitters in them. As defined in an article in *The Balance, and Columbian Repository* from 1806, a cocktail combines liquor, sugar, water, and bitters. While bitters aren't a requirement in the modern definition, they are critical for many drinks. Even a few dashes of these botanical-infused liquids can dramatically flavor a drink. Here are the kinds to know.

AROMATIC

One of the old standards, aromatic bitters are used for making drinks like Manhattans. The style is best known as the iconic Angostura brand, made since 1824, with its oversize paper label and yellow cap, and its flavor of baking spices with a quick sting of bitterness from gentian. Angostura isn't the only brand of aromatic bitters available these days, so keep an eye out at your specialty retailer if you want to try something different.

CREOLE

Cherry-red creole bitters are a floral counterpart to aromatic bitters. Peychaud's is the historic brand here, developed in New Orleans in 1830.

ORANGE

Another staple at most bars, orange bitters are made with dried citrus peels (which also contribute some bitterness) and often include coriander and cardamom.

Once you've got the basics down, feel free to branch out—almost any flavor you can think of is available in bitter form. Some are specific enough that they only work in a narrow category of drinks, but there are some wonderful bottles worth getting (such as chocolate, lavender, and celery) to help expand your cocktail ingredient palette.

021 { GET INTO MIXERS }

When we discuss mixers, we're not talking about those jugs of commercially made sweet-and-sour, margarita, or old-fashioned mix. Considering that the old-fashioned is a three-ingredient cocktail, the fact that there is a premix is a special kind of madness. Here are some actually useful mixers for stocking your bar.

SODAS

- Cola
- Lemon-lime
- Club*
- Seltzer*
- Ginger beer**
- Ginger ale**
- Tonic

MIXERS

- Tonic syrup
- Bloody Mary***
- Orgeat (almond syrup)
- Falernum (lime, clove, and ginger cordial)
- Grenadine
- Lime cordial

* Contrary to popular belief, seltzer and club soda are not the same. Seltzer is just carbonated water; club soda has salts of some kind, usually alkali ones like baking soda to offset the acidifying effect that carbonation has on water. They taste different and are used differently.

** Ginger beer is sometimes fermented and more potent (gingery), while ginger ale tends to be sweeter and lighter, often using only ginger extracts.

*** We'll show you how to make your own Bloody Mary in item 183, but it's not a terrible idea to have a mixer in case of a bad hangover.

022

GET HOOKED ON TONICS

All tonics are formulated with different botanical recipes, from floral to spiced, and mixing them with your favorite spirit will highlight different aspects. This means that your favorite gin or vodka may taste totally different when mixed with a new tonic. Choosing one from the huge variety available can be a little overwhelming—unless you see it as an opportunity to have friends over to conduct a taste-test.

BOTTLED Even if you favor tonic syrups, it's never a bad idea to have a couple of small bottles in the fridge. A great choice for those who like the feel of carbonation or the look of crystal clear beverages.

SYRUPS If you like less carbonation and don't mind some color in your gin and tonics, syrups are great. They also tend to be so flavorful that they taste good even without any alcohol, making them a fun choice for those on the wagon.

023 | PRODUCE THE JUICE

How much juice is there in each piece of fruit? Here's what you'll get out of each garden-variety, average-size citrus fruit.

LIME = 1 OZ JUICE

LEMON = 1½ OZ JUICE

ORANGE = 2½ OZ JUICE

GRAPEFRUIT = 3½ OZ JUICE

T Good for
hing and
ything—from
ks to drinking
e with tempered
nces

 **COCKTAIL** Shaken drinks like a Cosmopolitan (see item 134) or Lemon Drop (see item 137) get a classic cocktail glass. And just because it goes in this glass doesn't mean you need to add "-tini" to the

COUPE Coupe glasses were used for Champagne, originally, but are now popularly used for stirred and shaken classic drinks like a Daiquiri (see item 122).
5-8 ounces

024 | KNOW YOUR GLASSES SPECS

➵ Aside from the obvious need to contain liquids, glasses are critical to a good drink. They don't need to be fancy (bartenders often build their collections from thrift stores), but they should be appropriate for the drinks you want to make.

The shape will affect both the flavor and aroma of the drink, especially anything neat. Just for fun, try pouring a little of your favorite booze into a handful of differently shaped glasses, then smell and taste each one—they can differ dramatically.

Finally, size does matter: smaller is better (we're sure you've heard that before). Two small, cold, and freshly made cocktails are better than one huge drink that comes to room temperature halfway through. Plus, a standard-size cocktail in a big glass looks stingy and can lead to overserving guests.

OLD-FASHIONED Ideal for spirit-focused cocktails that may or may not come with ice, like the namesake Old Fashioned (see item 085), Sazerac (see item 097), and Negroni (see item 057). **10-12 ounces**

NICK AND NORA Martinis (see items 100-106) and other stirred drinks belong in these glasses, perfect for cocktail hour. **5 ounces**

COLLINS Drinks with soda, juices, or low-alcohol patio drinks such as a Pimm's Cup (see item 171), are best in a Collins glass. You'll need a bottle brush for washing the tall, narrow kind. **11 ounces**

CHAMPAGNE FLUTE Use flutes for Champagne and sparkling wine drinks like a Mimosa (see item 067), Bellini (see item 064), or Champagne cocktails. **5 ounces**

025 ✦ RAMP IT UP

➵ While not essential, some additional glassware items can be a lot of fun once you've got some shaking and stirring skills under your belt—and once you can identify the styles of cocktails that best suit your tastes.

These glasses, mugs, and novelty serving pieces are very much for the specialist or fetishist—you can certainly get away with using other mediums when you're just starting out. Wine glasses, for example, are workhorses and will do just fine for anything neat, such as whiskies, cordials, aperitifs, and after-dinner drinks.

A coffee mug works well for anything served hot, and a big bowl or even a hollowed-out pumpkin or watermelon makes an excellent punch bowl. Finally, simple pint glasses will do the job for tiki drinks and pretty much everything else.

But there's something deeply satisfying about drinking from a vessel made for a single type or category of cocktail, like a tin julep cup or a copper mug for your Moscow Mule. On a hot day there's nothing so cooling as frosty metal cup, and a Polynesian cocktail is even better in a mug with a tiki idol to ward off bad spirits.

WHISKY This shape amplifies aromas for neat spirits like brandies or whiskies. Stölzle Glencairn glass is the best. **6 ounces**

CORDIAL Cordials are small, curved glasses, perfect for a post-dinner shot of grappa, eau-de-vie, or liqueur. **3-4 ounces**

TIKI MUG You can serve anything tiki in these and they look dramatic. Heck, even juice is fun in one of these. **12-16 ounces**

JULEP CUP The gleaming silver cup for Mint Juleps (see item 176), the julep cup also works well with any drink that uses crushed ice. The tin keeps things cold and prevents dilution from happening too fast. **12 ounces**

COPPER MUG Mules (or bucks) including the Moscow Mule (see item 169), are the typical drink for classic copper, but anything with ice and soda works well in these vessels. **12-16 ounces**

PUNCH BOWL A big, glass bowl is great to have for entertaining and serving batched drinks or punches like the Fish House Punch (see item 250), and they're great for bustling parties. **Various sizes**

IRISH COFFEE MUG Irish Coffee (see item 194) and hot drinks deserve their namesake glass, along with layered drinks (see item 245). Made with tempered glass. **6-8 ounces**

WHISK(E)Y

TO "E" OR NOT TO "E"

FOR A SPIRIT THAT IS PRIMARILY DEFINED SIMPLY AS "ONE MADE FROM GRAIN," YOU'D IMAGINE THE COUNTLESS VARIATIONS TO BE STRAIGHTFORWARD AND COMPARABLE TO EACH OTHER—YET THE DISPARITY OFFERED BY THE VARYING AGES AND RECIPES SHOWS A REMARKABLE VERSATILITY. THE DIFFERENCES IN SPELLING ARE SIMPLY REGIONAL: "WHISKY" FOR SCOTCH, JAPANESE, AND CANADIAN; "WHISKEY" FOR ALL AMERICAN (INCLUDING BOURBON AND RYE) AND IRISH. IT IS COMMON TO SPELL IT "WHISK(E)Y" WHEN REFERRING TO ALL FORMS.

026

SIP A TASTE OF WHISK(E)Y

It is believed that Christian monks brought distillation to the British Isles somewhere around the 11th century, primarily as an alchemical process to distill herbal medicines made with local grain. Called *uisge beatha* (Gaelic for "water of life"), the drink was first historically noted when Henry II claimed Ireland in 1171 and described his army enjoying the spirit.

Eventually the practice of distillation evolved beyond the monasteries and apothecaries—farmers saw the process as a way to economize on grain bumper crop years, and the popularity of the practice (and the unaged grain liquor) surged. The tradition spread to Canada and the United States with Scottish and Irish immigrants in the 17th and 18th centuries.

027

SAY "OAK NO HE DIDN'T"

history

Scotch whisky as
an aged spirit wasn't
common until 1915, when
a teetotaling British prime
minister, David Lloyd George,
put the Immature Spirits
Act in place. While George
was hoping to slow the
consumption of the unaged
distilled grain liquor scourge
in Scotland, his law instead
kicked off the innovation and
experimentation with oak
aging now renown in
Scottish whiskies.

028

DECIPHER THE LABEL

Whisk(e)y labels often include a lot of descriptions and explanations that may not always make much sense. Here are some common phrases and what they really mean.

SINGLE MALT Single malts are distilled, aged, and bottled by one distillery and made entirely with malted grain of one kind (usually barley).

BLENDED MALT Two or more single malts from different distilleries combined together form a blended malt.

BLENDED WHISK(E)Y Blended whiskies are single or blended malts combined with a lighter grain spirit that may or may not be aged. Grain whiskies are made from less expensive and often unmalted grains (like corn) and distilled to a higher proof for more neutral flavors.

SINGLE CASK/BARREL Single-cask or single-barrel whiskies are bottled, as you may have guessed, from a single barrel.

CASK/BARREL STRENGTH These whiskies are not diluted with water after they're drawn from the barrel, but they may still be filtered unless otherwise stated. Note that unfiltered aged spirits may cloud slightly when chilled.

CASK FINISHED Cask finished whiskies get a secondary aging period in a different type of barrel, usually one that has previously aged something else, like port or sherry.

029 ⬥ COOK UP A WHISK(E)Y

STEP ONE The traditional methods for cooking whisk(e)y begin much in the same way as for beer: by malting barley. Grain is soaked in water, allowing it to germinate (an important step in which the enzyme amylase is created), and then roasted. Roasting over open peat fires incorporates the smoke character found in some Scotches.

STEP TWO The grain ingredients are combined to make a beer. The recipe (mashbill) is important and can define the style, as with bourbon, which requires at least 51 percent corn. Barley is often included even when it's not the primary grain, since the amylase enzyme converts starches from other grains into sugars accessible to the yeast.

STEP THREE Once the beer is ready, it's time to distill. The type of still and process used varies from product and distillery, from pot (lots of grain flavor) to continuous column distillation (higher proof with lighter flavors). On average, it takes 500 gallons of beer (at around 6 percent alcohol) to distill out 53 gallons—enough to fill a standard oak barrel.

STEP FOUR How and where the spirit is aged is where the art and distinction between whiskies comes in. The size of the barrel defines how much oak flavor is extracted—as does the location of the storage facility, the ambient temperature, and whether the barrel is new or used. Barrels that have previously aged sherry are especially sought after, due to their rich, nutty complexity.

STEP FIVE Bottling is more complex than simply dumping a bunch of barrels together. Each barrel, even those the same age and from the same location, will develop differently. The ratio of each barrel is important to the final product, just like when making a cocktail.

030 GET FRESH

The importance of fresh juices in your cocktails can't be stressed enough. Even in drinks where juice is merely a supporting player, having good, fresh juice is key. And in citrus drinks like margaritas, salty dogs, or mimosas, the freshness of the juice is critical and worth the extra effort. Particularly with citrus, the subtle oil fragrance can fade and end up tasting one-dimensional and acidic.

031 { **MAKE THINGS JUICY** }

Making juice at home is easier if you have the right tools, and not every juicer is right for every job. Here's a look at some of the most common tools.

	CITRUS SQUEEZER	Simple and effective, although they really only work on lemons and limes. In a pinch, cutting oranges or grapefruit into smaller pieces allows you to juice them with a squeezer.
	CITRUS REAMER	Those old-school reamers on which you twist the citrus are best left to larger oranges and grapefruit. Electric versions are available, and the handheld baton style is better for cooking situations than for cocktails.
	CITRUS PRESS	Expensive and unwieldy, these specialists combine the powers of the squeezer and the reamer, and make quick work of oranges and grapefruit.
	JUICER	Cold-press and extractors are great for juicing anything except soft and juicy produce, like watermelons, which leave behind a frightening puddle. Otherwise, they're great for anything you can think to put in there.
	BLENDER	You have to add water to make them work properly, but they do a better job with things like leafy herbs or juicy fruits.

032 | JUICE UP YOUR DRINKS

Freshness aside, not all juices are best made at home (and in some cases, are not reasonable to attempt). Here's our juice box filled with pulpy bits of information on all your favorites.

PEACH/APRICOT
Stone fruits will oxidize quickly, so be sure to mix in a little lemon or lime juice to help slow the process.

ORANGE/GRAPEFRUIT
These premade juices are of better quality than those for lemons or limes, but fresh juice is always worth the effort.

STRAWBERRY/BERRY
You can make syrup by cooking berries in a saucepan with sugar, then straining out the solids. If using a blender, combine chunks with water. Blend, then strain.

LEMON/LIME
Using a citrus squeezer is optimal because it releases citrus oils from the skin to help perfume to the juice.

PINEAPPLE
Those small tin cans of pineapple juice taste as much of metal as they do of fruit. Buy 100 percent pure juice in glass bottles if you can't make it yourself. In a blender, combine peeled chunks (core included!) with water. Blend, then strain.

POMEGRANATE
In the fall and early winter, you can often find fresh-pressed pomegranate juice at local farmers' markets.

WATERMELON
At the height of summertime, it's worth the effort to juice a watermelon—since it's so refreshing on its own. It's too juicy for a juicer, so combine peeled chunks into a blender with water. Blend, then strain.

TOMATO
What we think of as tomato juice is really more of a thin sauce. Juiced tomatoes just won't work in your Bloody Mary. Buy it.

CRANBERRY
This is really more of a beverage (sweetened with added sugar) than a juice. Buy it.

CARROT/BEET
Carrots and beets can add an earthiness to drinks, not to mention a striking bolt of color. Use a juicer if you can.

COCONUT
Unless you want to hone your machete skills, look for the cans of coconut milk sold at Asian markets or any of the countless new brands at your local store.

APPLE
Those big glass jugs of unfiltered apple juice or cider are decent if you don't have a juicer.

033 | CUSTOMIZE YOUR DRINKS

➤ Tailoring your cocktails with a little something extra is an easy and fun way to add a personal touch to your cocktails. Depending on the ingredients, there are a few ways to add them in. Simple syrups (see item 047), spirit infusions, tinctures, and shrubs are a couple of ways to incorporate fruits, herbs, and spices.

If you make infusions, keep track of your work by measuring and noting the amounts you use so that you can replicate them later. Tape the recipe onto the jar itself, and make sure you log the dates it went in and came out of infusion in your notes.

But just because you can add flavors to cocktails doesn't mean you should add all of them at once. Try adding one flavor at a time, and remember: Just like adding more wheels doesn't make a better car, adding more ingredients doesn't make a better cocktail.

INFUSE IT OR LOSE IT

034

Infusing a spirit is a fun way to add flavor to your favorite vodka, whiskey, or gin (really, any spirit will work). Fresh and dried fruits or vegetables, herbs, and fats are great choices for infusions. Mix a small amount, about a cup at a time, rather than whole bottles—the smaller volume allows you to experiment. It also lets you off the hook if something goes sideways and you end up making something that tastes like a sulfur mine. Here are two ways to do a proper infusion.

DIRECT INFUSION

STEP ONE In a mason jar, combine 1 cup of the spirit of your choice with the herbs, fruits, or vegetables you desire. Smaller pieces infuse faster, so get chopping, and don't include anything you wouldn't eat, like pits or cores. Fruit skins on apples and peaches have a lot of aroma and flavor, so be sure to leave those on. And go organic if you can—alcohol is a solvent and will infuse pesticides if you're not careful.

STEP TWO Shake it up, then store in a cool, dark place. Taste-test after a day, and give it another shake before putting it back. Fresh herbs will infuse in a couple of days, while denser fruits may take up to a week.

STEP THREE Strain out the solids (they look cool, but they'll dissolve and make a mess) and store the infused spirit in the fridge—when you're not slinging your apple-infused bourbon Manhattans.

FAT INFUSION

bacon

peanuts

popcorn

brown butter

STEP ONE Melt 1 ounce of the fat of your choice (if it's solid) at room temperature and combine with 1 cup of liquor in a small metal bowl or pot that will fit in your freezer. Stir the fat and spirit together to combine, cover, and allow to sit at room temperature for a few hours.

STEP TWO Place the fat-liquor combination in the freezer for at least a few hours (longer if the fat was liquid at room temperature).

STEP THREE Strain out the solid fats and put your infused spirits into a clean jar or bottle. Store in the fridge.

035 | FLAVOR WITH TINCTURES

Tinctures occupy a neat little groove of functionality: They're stronger in concentration than an infusion, and they're closer to bitters in terms of intensity. Think of using them to fine-tune the details. Herbs, spices, citrus peels, chile peppers, and other botanicals work best, as they allow you to control the intensity of each ingredient.

STEP ONE Fill a small jar halfway with high-proof vodka. Add your ingredients of choice (if using spices, toast them first), close the lid, and shake the jar to combine.

STEP TWO Place in a cool, dark location, and give the jar a shake every day or so, checking on the intensity and aroma. Don't be afraid to wait longer if it's not strong enough after a couple of weeks. Chiles might only take days, while spices could take weeks.

STEP THREE Once the desired strength is reached, remove the solids with a tea strainer. Pour the liquid into an eyedropper or bitters bottle for maximum control.

STEP FOUR Mix up some fun: Add a drop (or several) of your new tincture to your drink once it's mixed—it serves as a garnish and flavor enhancer in one!

036

SHRUB IT THE RIGHT WAY

An old colonial technique used to preserve fruits with vinegar and sugar, shrubs are a great way to add fresh fruit to cocktails via a tart syrup.

STEP ONE Cut your fruit into small pieces and combine 1 cup chopped fruit with 1 cup sugar. Lightly crush the fruit while you combine everything together. Cover and let rest in your fridge overnight.

STEP TWO Crush the fruit further and strain out the liquid. Make sure to extract as much juice as possible without pushing solids through the sieve.

STEP THREE Combine the strained juice with 1 cup vinegar and mix to combine.

STEP FOUR Now mix away, and remember a drink in the hand is worth two in the shrub.

SPHERES The low surface area of the sphere shape is designed to keep stirred cocktails or neat pours of spirits cold without overdiluting them.

CRUSHED Used for juleps, cobblers, and swizzles, crushed ice is used in cocktails with strong liquors that need to be chilled very quickly.

037 | PUT YOUR DRINK ON ICE

The ice shape, size, and amount you use to make and serve your drinks can all have a greater effect on the cocktail than you might imagine. In mixing, these factors determine temperature and dilution—both key elements to taste. In stirred drinks, a lack of dilution will make cocktails taste harsh, while too-small ice will make shaken or stirred drinks taste watered down. Here are a few variations to consider.

SPEARS Used to serve drinks in Collins glasses, spears of ice are both elegant and keep the cocktails perfectly fresh.

CUBED Cubes are the most common, all-purpose ice shape.

038

KEEP IT CLEAR

Making clear ice in your home freezer isn't as easy as it sounds—just look at one of your homemade cubes; they're likely cloudy from either bubbles or minerals. Despite the endless advice online about using purified or boiled water, it just isn't that simple. Writer and blogger Camper English has gone to extreme lengths with countless experiments on his site Alcademics.com, but the gist of his conclusions is that you need to freeze it directionally—top to bottom, like it would in a pond. To replicate this, he placed a small camping cooler in the freezer, which helped to slow down and change the direction of the freezing process. In the end, he only had to cut off the cloudy portion that formed at the bottom. The lesson? If you want clear ice, buy a block or large cube from your local bar—or just chill out and be cool with cloudy ice.

039 | BREAK THE ICE

For some advanced ice maneuvers, you'll need to add a few tools to your arsenal.

PICKS Used to shape ice, picks come in different styles to fit the job, from taking care of snitches (just kidding!) to forming spheres or breaking down large blocks into smaller, albeit irregular, chunks. It's old school, slow, and takes practice—but it also doesn't require plugs or maintenance.

KNIVES Paring and serrated knives can come in handy to shave away bumps to form smooth surfaces. Plus you probably already have one.

SAWS For heavy-duty ice work like breaking down whole 300-pound blocks, saws (in chain, hand, or band forms) make for quick and straight cuts.

MALLET AND CANVAS BAG Use a mallet and canvas bag to make crushed ice. Put the ice inside the canvas bag, then give it a good pounding. The canvas wicks away melting water, leaving snowy crushed ice inside the bag.

ICE BALL PRESS Presses take hunks of ice and turn them into perfect spheres. You open the two-part mold, add a chunk of ice to the bottom half, and replace the top half. The contraption quickly melts away the extraneous parts, leaving only the ice in the mold.

040 · COMMISSION AN ARTIST TO SCULPT PERFECT ICE

 In searching for a source of large, clear ice blocks, Beverage Director Ted Kilgore of Planter's House in St. Louis, Missouri, reached out to an ice sculpture company. When the company found out what Ted was really after—large specialty ice cubes for cocktails—they offered to sell him something even better than their uncarved blocks: ice precisely cut using their computer-automated machinery.

Now Ted can order the exact sizes and shapes he needs—such as cylinders perfectly matched to his barware—without adding the extra time and energy it would take to manually break down whole blocks. And the cost? About 50¢ each—more than making up the difference.

041 { DON'T BREAK THE MOLD }

For the sake of simplicity, you can't beat ice molds, which come in a staggering number of shapes. Want spheres? Large cubes? Hearts, stars, and horseshoes? They have a mold for that. The only problem with molds is that they're made of silicon, which is porous and will absorb odors from your freezer. Make sure you have a fresh box of baking soda in there, and once the ice is set, empty it out and store it in a zip-top bag. If the mold gets smelly, try soaking it in a vinegar-water solution.

042 | GET JIGGER HAPPY

f you only remember one piece of nformation from this book, let it be this: Measure your ingredients. Keep this in mind and it will serve you well.

Particularly in the beginning, it's mportant to take your time and measure out the ingredients as best you can. You'll be more likely to have good, balanced drinks that you can make repeatedly with the same results.

There are quite a few measuring tools to choose from; use what speaks to you. A few may have steep learning curves, but, as they say, you can't make a flip (see item 195) without breaking a few eggs.

043 | MEASURE TWICE, MIX ONCE

Once you pick your preferred measuring method, remember to take your time. It's better to be accurate than to be fast. Like everything, speed comes with time and practice. Discussions among bartenders about the accuracy of particular brands or styles of tools always get heated, and rightly so—a small error in your tools when making a cocktail can throw the drink off balance. As a beginner, it's more important for you to be consistent with your tools than for them to be precise.

Ultimately, what matters most in the recipes are the ratios, and you can only go so far talking about accuracy before it becomes a philosophical discussion about imperfection and absolute truths, platonic ideals, and infinity. Stay out of that rabbit

DOUBLE-SIDED JIGGER Essentially tiny measuring cups, the smaller end of a double-sided jigger typically holds half the amount of the larger end. The nicer models have incremental measurements etched inside the cup. A word of caution: due to their V shape, it's nearly impossible to eyeball a small amount, and they can be easy to spill. Practice with water until you get comfortable.

POUR SPOUTS You'll sometimes see bartenders pouring directly into a glass using a technique called free-pouring—they "count" the amount of liquid as they pour. This technique, while accurate and blazing fast in the right hands, takes lots of practice. If you're serious about it, get some pour spouts and practice with water.

MEASURING CUP Another popular choice are mini measuring cups, which have marks for a variety of measurements, from ounces and milliliters to tablespoons and fractions of a cup. OXO makes the most popular version, with an angled edge inside that allows you to see the fill marks while looking down at the cup. The only problem is that many don't have a $\frac{1}{3}$ ounce measurement.

MEASURING SPOONS For more precise or oddball tiny measurements, measuring spoons can come in handy. Measuring out 2 teaspoons gives you $\frac{1}{3}$ ounce, $\frac{1}{2}$ tablespoon (or $1\frac{1}{2}$ teaspoons) equals $\frac{1}{4}$ ounce, and 1 tablespoon is $\frac{1}{2}$ ounce. It's not the fastest way to measure for cocktails, but it's good to know.

BARSPOON On occasion you'll see an old recipe calling for a barspoon of something, which is 5 ml ($\frac{1}{6}$ oz). The problem is that most barspoons don't hold that exact amount. If you really want to use yours to measure, make sure you test out the true amount of liquid it holds. In a pinch, a teaspoon holds close to 5 ml.

044

ACCESSORIZE YOUR BAR

If you already have the basic set of bar tools (see item 005) and have shaken a few drinks, here are a few more pieces of helpful equipment you might want to consider.

ICE TONGS
It seems like a small thing, but adding ice to a glass or grabbing a cherry without freezing your hands (or getting them sticky) is nice. Plus it makes you look like you know what you're doing.

ICE BUCKETS
If you entertain a lot, getting a couple of ice buckets (or other waterproof containers) will make your life a lot easier. Designate one for "dirty ice," (to hold bottles of juice, sparkling wine, or beer). The second holds "clean ice," which you'll use to mix with and serve in drinks.

GIANT ICE CUBE MOLD
Your basic freezer ice is usually fine for mixing and stirring drinks, but a modest investment in a few nice ice molds can make a huge difference when serving.

LEWIS ICE BAG & WOODEN MALLET
These are great tools if you make or drink a lot of juleps or swizzles. They're even good for serving oysters or shrimp cocktail (the food, not some crazy drink). Bonus points for the stress relief of smashing the heck out of something with a mallet.

WOODEN MUDDLER

Look for large, hardwood versions that aren't coated in lacquer (coatings will chip off). Grabbing it by the handle, you should feel a nice amount of weight, like a little club—perfect for whacking those clumps in bags of ice.

BAR MAT

If you're mixing a lot of drinks, a bar mat is helpful for containing drips. It's amazing how much liquid it can hold, which is awesome until you try to move a floppy mat full of liquid across the kitchen to the sink. Save yourself some grief by placing the mat over a cutting board so you can safely support it all.

045 COVER YOUR ASSETS WITH COASTERS

When putting your bar together, don't forget the humble coaster. Simple and commonplace in bars and pubs, coasters are even more important at home, where nice furniture can quickly be ruined by dripping condensation. Even some stone and metal surfaces benefit from the fearless protection of coasters, as citric acid in mixed drinks can react and leave rings on their surfaces. Availability in a huge range of styles and materials means there's a coaster design for everyone's home décor, and they're cheaper than having to get something refinished. The coaster's clear.

046 | CHOOSE YOUR FAMILY INGREDIENTS

You'll see that many recipes share common ratios, and appear related—they often are. By swapping one ingredient for something similar (such as a different spirit or sweetener) you can have a completely different cocktail. In no other category is this more true than with sours. Every cocktail listed basically has the same three ingredients: two parts spirit, ¾ part citrus, and ¾ part sweet. These ratios are starting points:

Citrus acidity, the strength of your simple syrup, and the choice of liquor may require less or more of one thing or another. One powerful recipe can create more than 16 drinks and make you feel like a wizard behind the bar. In Chapter 2, you'll find our preferred recipes for some of these drinks, in different ratios (we like them less sweet, showcasing more of the spirit's flavor), but these are just guidelines. Make them suit your taste.

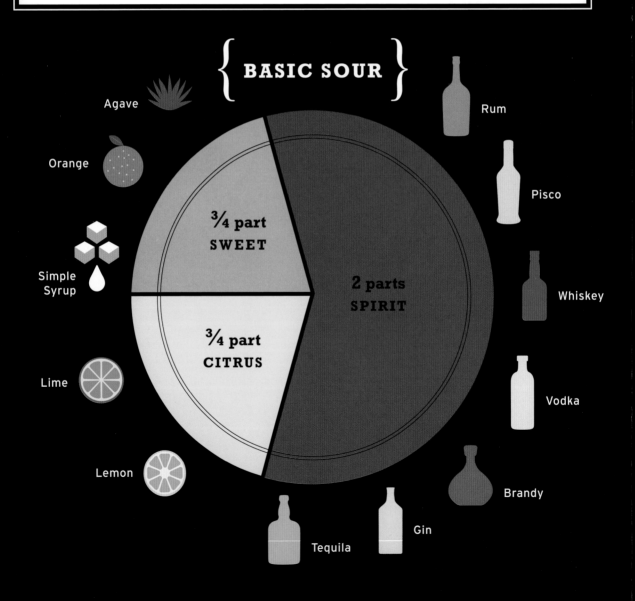

{ BASIC SOUR }

Agave

Orange

Simple Syrup

Lime

Lemon

Tequila

Gin

Brandy

Vodka

Whiskey

Pisco

Rum

¾ part SWEET

¾ part CITRUS

2 parts SPIRIT

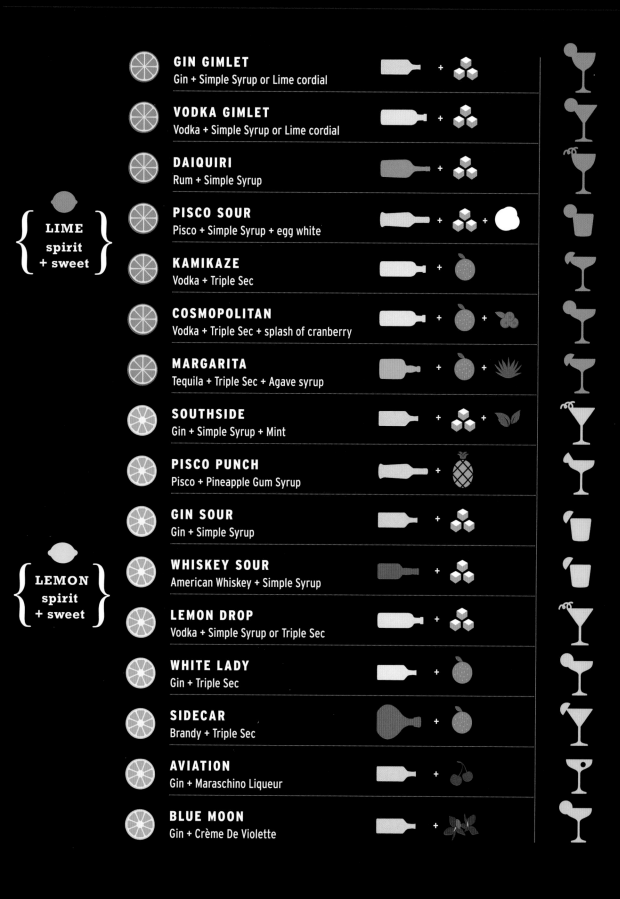

LIME
spirit + sweet

GIN GIMLET
Gin + Simple Syrup or Lime cordial

VODKA GIMLET
Vodka + Simple Syrup or Lime cordial

DAIQUIRI
Rum + Simple Syrup

PISCO SOUR
Pisco + Simple Syrup + egg white

KAMIKAZE
Vodka + Triple Sec

COSMOPOLITAN
Vodka + Triple Sec + splash of cranberry

MARGARITA
Tequila + Triple Sec + Agave syrup

SOUTHSIDE
Gin + Simple Syrup + Mint

PISCO PUNCH
Pisco + Pineapple Gum Syrup

LEMON
spirit + sweet

GIN SOUR
Gin + Simple Syrup

WHISKEY SOUR
American Whiskey + Simple Syrup

LEMON DROP
Vodka + Simple Syrup or Triple Sec

WHITE LADY
Gin + Triple Sec

SIDECAR
Brandy + Triple Sec

AVIATION
Gin + Maraschino Liqueur

BLUE MOON
Gin + Crème De Violette

047 | KEEP IT SIMPLE

Simple syrup, as the name indicates, is by far one of the easiest and most versatile ways to introduce sweetness to beverages—alcoholic or not. Sweetening iced tea or coffee is much easier when the sugar is already dissolved in water, and this easy ingredient is crucial to good cocktails. There are two basic recipes: Standard simple is equal parts sugar and water, while rich simple doubles the amount of sugar at a ratio of two parts sugar to one part water.

SIMPLE SYRUP

1 part sugar, 1 part water

 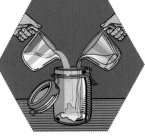

•➔ STOVETOP METHOD

Combine sugar and water in a small saucepan. Cook over medium heat and stir until dissolved. Cover and allow to cool, then refrigerate. Will keep for about 3 weeks.

•➔ CONTAINER METHOD

Combine sugar and water in a bottle, mason jar, or kitchen container. Shake to combine, let rest for a few minutes, then repeat the shaking-rest cycle until all the crystals dissolve.

RICH SIMPLE SYRUP

2 parts sugar, 1 part water

•➔ STOVETOP METHOD

Combine sugar and water in a small saucepan. Cook over medium heat and stir until dissolved. Allow to cool, then refrigerate. Will keep for about 6 months.

048

CHOOSE YOUR SWEETENER

The type of sugar you use in your simple syrup will affect your drink, so choose wisely.

•➔ **GRANULATED** Standard granulated sugar is the most versatile, letting you tweak the sweetness of cocktails without changing the flavor.

•➔ **UNREFINED** Brown and unrefined sugars have more of a molasses flavor, increasing in intensity from golden brown sugar to "raw" (turbinado or demerara) and the powerfully flavored *muscovado*, *piloncillo*, and *jaggery*.

•➔ **NECTAR** Honey or agave nectar can also be used to make simple syrups. Honey works especially well with fall flavors and hot drinks, and agave is an alternative for those watching their sugar intake—it's sweeter than cane sugars, so adjust appropriately!

049 { REFINE YOUR SUGAR SYRUPS }

The best part of simple syrup is that it can act as a blank canvas for customization—add your own garden herbs or favorite spices to concoct some excellent cocktail combinations. Use the stovetop method of the standard 1:1 recipe for these, and, if desired, strain out the solids before refrigerating.

FLAVOR	HOW MUCH	WHEN	NOTES
Spices (cinnamon, cloves)	2 tablespoons fresh spices per 1 cup sugar	Add with water and sugar	Spices can be powdered (about 1 tablespoon per cup of sugar) although the syrup may be gritty
Vanilla	½ bean per 1 cup sugar	Add with water and sugar	You can also use leftover scraped vanilla pods
Tea	1 tablespoon loose tea or 2 teabags per 1 cup sugar	Add with water and sugar	Strain carefully to remove any sediment
Dried flowers (lavender, hibiscus)	1 tablespoon per 1 cup sugar	Add with water and sugar	Strain carefully to remove any sediment
Citrus	Peel from 1 lemon, 1 orange, 2 limes, or half a large grapefruit per 1 cup sugar	After the syrup has been removed from heat	Strain out peels before storing in the fridge to avoid bitterness
Ginger	4 ounces washed and unpeeled sliced ginger per 1 cup sugar	After the syrup has been removed from heat	You can make an uncooked version by blending the ingredients together, then straining
Herbs (mint, basil, etc.)	Varies by herb, but about ½ cup of leafy herbs to ¼ cup woodier herbs, stems and all, per 1 cup sugar	After the syrup has been removed from heat	Herbs will get vegetal if you cook them, so let the syrup cool slightly before adding mint or basil

AGAVE

IT'S UNKNOWN IF THE DISTILLATION OF AGAVE SPIRITS WAS HAPPENING BEFORE THE ARRIVAL OF THE SPANISH IN THE 16TH CENTURY, BUT THE FERMENTATION OF AGAVE BY ROASTING IN THE EARTH CERTAINLY WAS.

050

GET THE HISTORY

➤ As the story goes, the fermentable sweetness in agave was discovered when lighting struck an agave plant, allowing access to the sugars trapped inside. How electrifying.

The core of the agave is filled with fibrous strands, plus polysaccharides like insulin. When heated, the long chains of stored energy break down into sugars, such as fructose, which can be digested by yeasts to create alcohol.

As the Spanish crown forbid the colonists in Mexico from producing wine and brandy (for fear of undercutting the export economy of the homeland), the Spanish instead encouraged distillation, and the first tequila distillery popped up in what is now Jalisco in the early 17th century. Mezcal and other varieties remained mostly regional products, even as tequila began to be exported in the late 19th century.

Call it a Hollywood ending (or, in this case, beginning), but agave spirit exports and familiarity with them outside of Mexico remained modest until Prohibition made it fashionable (and relatively easy) for the Hollywood elite to travel to Mexico to party.

After World War II, tourism and the thirst for agave soared, fueled by the margarita. It took another 60 years for mezcal and more regional spirits to earn acclaim outside of the rural villages where they are made. We'll drink to that.

051

MEET AGAVE'S RELATIVE

Everyone thinks of agave as a type of cactus, but it is in fact a member of the asparagaceae family—a group of flowering plants that includes asparagus. Thankfully, agave spirits don't make your pee smell funny.

With few exceptions, all agave-based spirits have a similar process for making the ferment and distilling it.

•➜ **STEP ONE** Agave is harvested from farms or out in the hills where it grows wild. The sharp outer leaves are removed until it resembles a pineapple (or *piña*).

•➜ **STEP TWO** The *piñas* are cooked. For tequila, they are mostly steamed in large ovens or autoclaves. But for mezcal and other spirits, they are often cooked in stone-lined pits that are heated with wood; they cook, buried, for several days.

•➜ **STEP THREE** Once cooked, the agave gets crushed in a modern roller mill or by a large stone wheel called a tahona.

•➜ **STEP FOUR** The crushed agave is mixed with water, and, while it's common to remove the solids when fermenting tequila, the other varieties usually skip that step, allowing wild yeast to ferment the mix. The ferment is then double-distilled in pot stills.

053

TYPECAST YOUR TEQUILA

When discussing agave, your mind may go to only one place: tequila. And while that's a fine spirit to focus on, make sure you've got your details straight—and don't forget about its lovely agave cousins.

TEQUILA The most common of the agave spirits, tequila is made exclusively from the blue agave variety called *Tequila Webber*. All tequila must contain at least 51 percent distilled agave spirit, but the best-quality ones use 100 percent agave and may only be produced in Jalisco, Michoacán, Nayarit, Tamaulipas, and Guanajuato. Tequila can be *blanco* (unaged or rested for less than 2 months), *reposado* (aged at least 2 months but not more than 1 year), *añejo* (aged at least 1 year but not more than 3), or *extra-añejo* (aged at least 3 years). In Mexico it is typically drunk neat with a chaser of *sangrita*, a fruit and chile juice that sometimes contains tomato.

MEZCAL Mezcal can be made from some 50 different known varieties of agave, although a good amount of mezcal is made from the *espadín* type. While we think of mezcal primarily coming from Oaxaca, it can also be made in Durango, Guanajuato, Guerrero, Michoacán, San Luis Potosí, Puebla, Tamaulipas, and Zacatecas. Often smoky from the firepit cooking process, this rustic cousin to tequila can have lots of herbal and fruit flavors. It's traditionally consumed with orange wedges sprinkled with ground chiles and salt.

BACANORA Made with *espadín* in the northern state of Sonora, *bacanora* is often cooked in pits like mezcal. The flavor is milder, however, and in more limited quantities. Illegal until 1992, *bacanora* was traditionally considered a product for locals.

RAICILLA The name *raicilla* is based on the word *raíz*, which translates to "roots"—perhaps a nod to the old way of making spirits in Jalisco, before tequila became an industry. Made mostly from the agaves *maximiliana* and *inaequidens*, it's best to treat this spirit like you would moonshine—carefully.

SOTOL In Chihuahua, Coahuila, and Durango, *sotol* is made from an evergreen bush (within the same family as agave) called "Dessert Spoon"—which takes about 15 years to grow and produces approximately one bottle per plant harvested.

Recipes & Techniques

———◆———

It's possible you opened the book in order to get to this chapter—the recipes, which contain a mix of classic cocktails and modern recipes sourced from USBG bartenders across the country. This chapter is the vanilla filling to the chocolate cookies on either side—instructions for instant gratification.

This collection is by no means meant to be exhaustive; it instead offers a foundation for the craft of cocktail making. You'll learn how to make many drinks using one magic ratio, when to customize your existing knowledge with infusions and substitutions, and proper techniques for making everything taste as good as it gets.

Your taste, preferred spirit brands, and style of mixing will all affect the cocktail you stir up. Fine-tune the measurements to suit your needs; ultimately, everyone likes their drinks a little different. That's the beauty of bartending at home: Your drink is made exactly the way you like it.

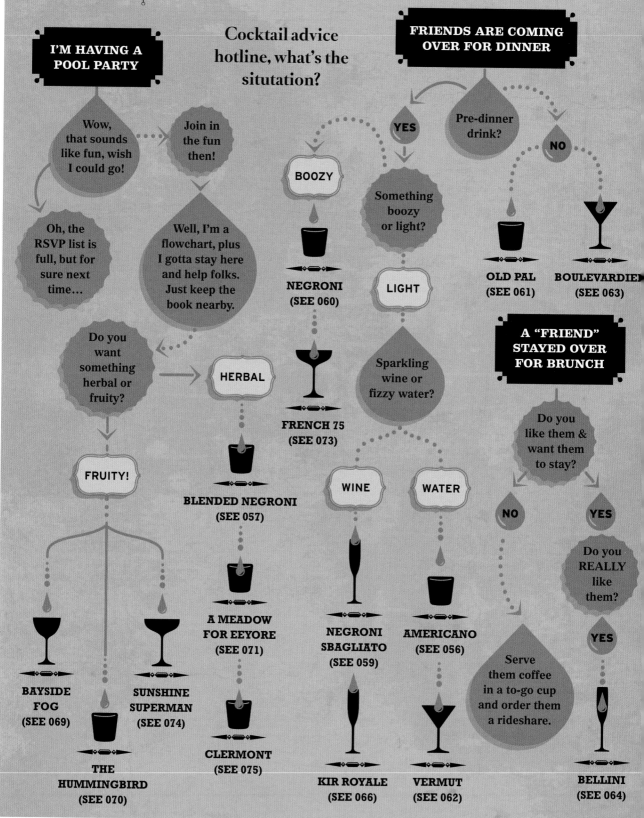

055

APPRECIATE APERITIVOS

Aperitivos, or aperitif cocktails, can take some getting used to, especially for the uninitiated. They're dosed with bitter herbs like wormwood, roots such as gentian, or other botanicals like cinchona bark or citrus peels, which have the purported effect of stimulating the appetite.

056

THE AMERICANO

Vermouths, which are wines infused with botanicals, and bitter liqueurs, such as Campari, are common ingredients in predinner drinks in Europe, so it makes sense that someone would combine the two. Like much in the bar world, there are conflicting stories about the name of the Americano: some say it comes from the Italian word *amer* (Italian for bitter) and others say it was named after Americans enjoying the drink. One thing we can agree on: it's delicious.

1 oz sweet vermouth

1 oz Campari

1½ oz seltzer water

Lemon or orange slice to garnish

In a highball glass with ice, add the vermouth, Campari, and seltzer. Stir to combine and garnish with a citrus slice.

057 { CLASSIC NEGRONI }

The most widely told legend of the birth of this cocktail is that Count Camillo Negroni, of Florence, Italy, asked his bartender to use gin in place of the seltzer water in his Americano. The equal parts of each ingredient make it a simple but effective masterpiece.

1½ oz gin

1½ oz sweet vermouth

1½ oz Campari

Orange slice to garnish

•→ *Combine all ingredients except garnish in a rocks glass with ice. Stir to combine and garnish with an orange slice.*

058 ◈ SERVE IT UP

Sometimes you want a more potent and refined version of the Negroni, and the drink works equally well served up in a coupe or cocktail glass. Use the same recipe, but substitute an orange twist for the orange slice. Combine in an ice-filled mixing glass and stir 20–30 seconds, until well chilled. Strain the cocktail into a chilled glass; garnish with the orange twist.

059

MAKE IT WRONG

➤→ The *Negroni Sbagliato* (which translates from Italian to "Wrong Negroni") is a lighter variation that substitutes sparkling wine for the gin. It makes a great predinner drink if you're planning on serving or drinking a lot of wine with dinner, or on those days when you would rather take it easy.

USBG | SAN FRANCISCO CHAPTER

✦ JOHN CODD ✦

General Manager | Tradition

060

MAKE IT REALLY WRONG

➤→ Bartender John Codd wasn't looking to innovate on the classic Negroni cocktail when he decided to see what would happen if you blended it, but the results are wonderfully light, less bitter, and more citrusy.

Fix the classic recipe (see item 057) and throw the whole thing, ice and all, into a blender. Blend until it's a light pink slushie treat.

061 | EMBRACE AN OLD PAL

Harry MacElhone was a Scotsman who worked as a bartender in New York. He then moved to Paris and opened "Harry's New York Bar" during Prohibition. He's credited with creating two interesting Negroni variations that are worth trying out. From his 1922 book, *ABC of Mixing Cocktails*, the Old Pal dials down the sweetness of a Negroni and kicks up the flavor by using an aged spirit. The Old Pal is a great example of how different a cocktail can become with a couple of modifications.

1½ oz rye whiskey or a high-rye Canadian whisky

1½ oz dry vermouth

1½ oz Campari

•→ *Combine all ingredients in an ice-filled mixing glass and stir 20–30 seconds, until well chilled. Strain the cocktail into a chilled glass.*

062

VARY YOUR VERMOUTH

DRY/FRENCH

For classic martinis, this vermouth is a must—with light, bright herbal flavors that also make it great for cooking.

SWEET/ITALIAN

Spices dominate this style of vermouth with a reddish-amber color that often comes from caramel.

BIANCO/BLANC

A sweeter take on the herbal dry vermouth, *bianco* or *blanc* vermouth boasts a touch more botanical intensity.

---

063 { THE BOULEVARDIER }

Another Negroni variation from MacElhone, this one from his 1927 book *Barflies and Cocktails*, the Boulevardier sticks closer to the original. Although, given that Prohibition was firmly in place in the United States, it's hard to say if MacElhone was showing off his good fortune in bourbon whiskey or if it was wishful thinking.

1½ oz bourbon whiskey

1½ oz sweet vermouth

1½ oz Campari

•→ *Combine all ingredients in an ice-filled mixing glass and stir 20–30 seconds, until well chilled. Strain the cocktail into a chilled glass.*

•→ *Note: Some folks like to dial back both the vermouth and Campari in this drink to let the whiskey shine as the primary flavor, but it works great in MacElhone's equal-parts ratio.*

064

THE BELLINI

This simple mix of puréed white peaches and sparkling wine comes from 1940s Venice, Italy. Bartender Giuseppe Cipriani named the drink after the 15th-century Venetian painter Giovanni Bellini for the similarity of the drink's color to the artist's work.

2 oz peach pureé (yellow peach pureé can be used if white peaches aren't available)

4 oz sparkling wine

•◗ Add the purée to a flute, then add the sparkling wine. Give it a gentle, quick stir with a barspoon, and serve.

•◗ Note: If making your own pureé from fresh peaches, adjust the sweetness with simple syrup and tartness with lemon juice.

065

CRACK SOME BUBBLY

When using sparkling wine in cocktails, stick to something cheap and cheerful that you wouldn't mind drinking on its own. Italian prosecco, French *cremant*, Spanish *cava*, or just plain old "sparkling wine" all work; choose something on the dry side whenever possible, especially in sweet drinks.

⇢ STEP ONE Remove the foil and, while pointing the cork toward the ceiling or other safe direction and keeping a hand or thumb on top, remove the wire cage by untwisting the loop at the bottom.

⇢ STEP TWO Place a kitchen towel or napkin over the cork and hold it with one hand, while you gently twist the bottle with your dominant hand. You should feel the cork start to move upward until you get a nice "pop."

⇢ STEP THREE Pour into glasses, keeping the towel or napkin handy to catch drips. Then raise a toast!

066 KIR ROYALE

While crème de cassis (currant liqueur) is traditional in the *kir royale*, this recipe is also a great way to enjoy your collection of fruit liqueurs and crèmes.

½ oz crème de cassis

5 oz sparkling wine

 Add the crème de cassis to a flute, then add the sparkling wine. Give it a gentle, quick stir with a barspoon, and serve.

067

THE MIGHTY MIMOSA

You can easily substitute most sweet citrus juices for the orange juice—who needs Bloody Marys for brunch when you can have Blood Orange Mimosas, instead?

2 oz orange juice

4 oz sparkling wine

⇢ *Add the juice to a flute, then top with the sparkling wine.*

068

GO ON THE SPRITZ

Combining both sparkling and bitter flavors, spritzes (German for "sparkling" and "splash") are traditionally a combination of sparkling wine, bitter liqueur, and sparkling water. The tradition is said to have been developed in the 1800s in the Italian state of Veneto, where foreigners—who were unaccustomed to the strength of the local wines—would ask for them diluted with a spritz of water.

069

BAYSIDE FOG

The Bayside Fog is an homage to the local cranberries grown in foggy bogs along the coast of Oregon—accented with long pepper, one of Kate Bolton's favorite flavors (like a fragrant black pepper). The tincture gives the drink a spicy pop.

1½ oz Aperol (or other aperitivo-style liqueur)

½ oz Clear Creek cranberry liqueur

2 teaspoons long pepper tincture (see item 035, use 25 grams finely ground long pepper)

3 oz seltzer water

Add the Aperol, cranberry liqueur, and tincture to a wine glass, then top with seltzer water. Give it a gentle, quick stir with a barspoon and garnish with an orange twist.

070 THE HUMMINGBIRD

Named for the bright red nectar used in hummingbird feeders, this drink is a play on bitters and soda, enriched with vanilla and coffee. Cappelletti is less bitter than other Italian aperitivos, making for an elegant drink that won't clip your wings.

1½ oz Cappelletti aperitivo

1 teaspoon vanilla extract

1 teaspoon coffee tincture (see item 035, use a 1:2 ratio of whole coffee beans to liquid)

3 oz seltzer water

Long lemon twist, made with channel knife (see item 256)

•➔ Add the Cappelletti, vanilla, and tincture to a rocks or old-fashioned glass, then top with seltzer water. Give it a gentle, quick stir with a barspoon and garnish with the lemon twist.

071 { A MEADOW FOR EEYORE }

The woodsy flavors from the herbal vermouth, chamomile, and honey in this drink are so evocative of a lovely rolling meadow that it would brighten up even Pooh's glum companion.

1½ oz Imbue Petal & Thorn vermouth

½ oz honey syrup (1:1)

1 teaspoon chamomile tincture (see item 035, use 25 grams dried chamomile flowers)

3 oz tonic water

Lime wheel

Seasonal edible flower or flowering herb sprig

•➔ Add the vermouth, honey syrup, and tincture to a rocks or old-fashioned glass, and top with tonic water. Give it a gentle, quick stir with a barspoon and garnish with the lime wheel and, for an extra flourish, a flower or sprig.

✦ MARTÍN TUMMINO ✦

Bar Manager | Art Bar

072

ANARANJADITO

Based on the classic Argentinean Coloradito (which means "reddish" in Spanish), this drink (which translates to "orange-ish") is like an Americano but with dry vermouth and without seltzer, getting its signature hue from the lighter, Aperol-style aperitivo. This cocktail is meant to be enjoyed alongside a picada, the Argentinean assortment of cured meats, cheeses, olives, and other small bites.

2 oz dry vermouth

1 oz aperitivo (like Aperol)

1 lemon slice

Lemon peel

⊷ *Combine vermouth, aperitivo, and lemon slice in a cocktail shaker with ice. Shake hard 8–10 seconds and pour into a rocks or old-fashioned glass. Express lemon swath over drink and drop the peel in the drink.*

PAUL JOHNSEN ✦ USBG South Regional VP

073 FRENCH 75

Created around the first World War, this elegant drink was said to pack the wallop of a 75mm French artillery shell.

1½ oz gin

½ oz lemon juice

½ oz simple syrup (1:1)

3 dashes citrus bitters (such as Bittermen's Boston Bittahs)

2 lemon peels

Brut sparkling wine

⊷ *Combine gin, lemon juice, simple syrup, bitters, and one of the lemon peels in a cocktail shaker with ice. Shake hard 8–10 seconds, and strain into a cold coupe or champagne flute. Top with sparkling wine. Express the remaining lemon peel over the drink and garnish with peel in the drink.*

MATT COWAN ✦ Cocktail Curator | La Cour

074 ◈ SUNSHINE SUPERMAN

This drink is sunshine in a glass, perfect for summer barbecues. It also works in the dead of winter to warm you up from the inside—you'll be visualizing those summer nights in no time.

1 oz mezcal or gin (your choice)

½ oz lemon juice

½ oz aperitivo (like Aperol)

½ oz grapefruit liqueur (Giffard Pamplemousse preferred)

1 oz prosecco sparkling wine

Grapefruit peel

⊷ *Combine spirit, lemon juice, aperitivo, and liqueur in a shaker with ice. Shake 8–10 seconds and strain into a cold coupe or flute. Top with sparkling wine. Express the grapefruit peel over the drink and drop the peel in the glass.*

075

CLERMONT

This vegetal, bittersweet, and fizzy drink is a great way to start an afternoon. The rhubarb infusion is an excellent bonus, adding a layer of that tangy flavor in cocktails where the vermouth is the star.

1½ oz dry vermouth infused with rhubarb

¾ oz Cynar (artichoke amaro liqueur)

¾ oz Cocchi Americano *Rosa* (rosé aperitif wine)

Brut sparkling wine

Fresh rhubarb stalk

•➜ *For the infused vermouth: In a large jar combine one 375 ml bottle of dry vermouth with 1½ stalks of rhubarb, roughly chopped. Let it infuse in the refrigerator for three days, then strain and store in the fridge until ready to use.*

•➜ *Fill an old-fashioned or rocks glass with ice and add the vermouth, Cynar, and Cocchi, and then top with sparkling wine. Stir gently. Shave a curl of rhubarb with a vegetable peeler and garnish.*

CHOOSE YOUR SPIRIT FORWARD DRINK

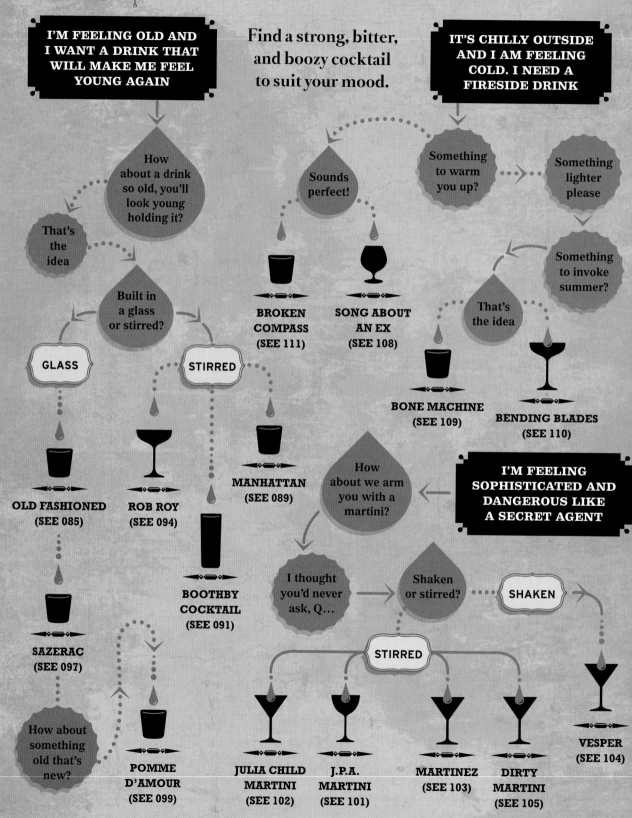

I'M FEELING OLD AND I WANT A DRINK THAT WILL MAKE ME FEEL YOUNG AGAIN

Find a strong, bitter, and boozy cocktail to suit your mood.

IT'S CHILLY OUTSIDE AND I AM FEELING COLD. I NEED A FIRESIDE DRINK

How about a drink so old, you'll look young holding it?

That's the idea

Sounds perfect!

Something to warm you up?

Something lighter please

Built in a glass or stirred?

Something to invoke summer?

That's the idea

BROKEN COMPASS (SEE 111)

SONG ABOUT AN EX (SEE 108)

GLASS

STIRRED

BONE MACHINE (SEE 109)

BENDING BLADES (SEE 110)

OLD FASHIONED (SEE 085)

ROB ROY (SEE 094)

MANHATTAN (SEE 089)

How about we arm you with a martini?

I'M FEELING SOPHISTICATED AND DANGEROUS LIKE A SECRET AGENT

BOOTHBY COCKTAIL (SEE 091)

I thought you'd never ask, Q…

Shaken or stirred?

SHAKEN

SAZERAC (SEE 097)

STIRRED

How about something old that's new?

POMME D'AMOUR (SEE 099)

JULIA CHILD MARTINI (SEE 102)

J.P.A. MARTINI (SEE 101)

MARTINEZ (SEE 103)

DIRTY MARTINI (SEE 105)

VESPER (SEE 104)

077 | GET A KICK IN THE GLASS

>>→ A mixing glass is best for dark, potent cocktails, gently stirred with a spoon rather than the kinetic energy of a shaker. A pour spout is a nice touch, and make sure that your strainer fits in the mouth.

Some folks prefer beakers for their aesthetic appeal and sturdy nature, but a pint glass will do, or even a glass measuring cup—it won't impress many guests, but a cold cocktail always will.

078 | BE THE BIG SPOON

>>→ Barspoons come in all styles, some with decorative elements or tools on the handle, like garnish forks or muddlers. Some aren't even spoons but have a smooth rounded tip at both ends. A barspoon without a spoon might sound like a faulty piece of equipment, but the spoon itself doesn't help stir the drink. What you want is something to stir the contents without causing the ice to chip. Plus, not having a spoon end allows you to easily stir drinks built in a glass, such as a Pimm's Cup (see item 171).

DON'T STIR UP TROUBLE

Stirring a drink isn't rocket science (you add your booze, ice, and stir), but there are a few things to keep in mind that can make your drinks better.

ICE Use whole ice cubes, and use plenty of them.

TIME Make sure you stir for a long enough period (20–30 seconds, which may be longer than you think).

EASE The spoon, ice, and cocktail should all be moving as one. Calmly. Quietly. If you're swishing the spoon around or making your ice clank, just stop, take a deep breath, and stir.

080

CRACK UP YOUR COCKTAIL

Stirred drinks tend to be boozier, so it may seem counterintuitive to ensure proper dilution. But the water is just as important as the ice. Dilution gives the cocktail balance, especially when using higher-ABV spirits. If your drinks are too powerful, try adding cracked ice. Place an ice cube on the palm of your hand and use a quick whack with the back of your barspoon to break it into smaller pieces. Add those chunks along with regular ice and enjoy the properly mellowed results.

GIN

IN ORDER TO BE CONSIDERED GIN, THE SPIRIT MUST BE FLAVORED WITH JUNIPER BERRIES, AND IT'S USUALLY MADE WITH NEUTRAL GRAIN DISTILLATE (ESSENTIALLY VODKA) DISTILLED WITH A HOST OF BOTANICALS THAT OFTEN INCLUDE CITRUS, SPICES, AND HERBS. IN FACT, SOME BARTENDERS EVEN REFER TO GIN AS JUNIPER-FLAVORED VODKA.

081

LEARN THE HISTORY

Gin has a storied and sometimes scandalous background that traces many countries and time periods.

By some accounts, Italian monks were adding juniper to their booze a millennium ago, but it's mainly thought that the spirit (then known as genever) was being distilled as far back as 16th-century Holland. Indeed, the term "Dutch courage" apparently began as a reference to the feeling of fearlessness after drinking a shot of genever, and it's thought to have come from British

soldiers fighting in the Dutch War of Independence (also known as the Eighty Years War) during the 1500s.

As time went on, the Dutch popularized gin as a medical tonic (juniper being a natural diuretic), and it became popular in England when William of Orange took the British throne during the last part of the 17th century.

During the next hundred years, the English had their ups and downs with the spirit, from the boom of the Gin Craze in the 18th century (when the government allowed the unlicensed production of gin) to the bust of the Gin Act years later, which sought to temper the effects of this cheap "Mother's Ruin."

It wasn't until the 19th century, with the invention of the continuous still, that today's style of London Dry gin was developed and popularized.

082

PLUCK A BERRY

The small berries of the juniper bush were thought to be medicinal in the 17th century, and so they were prescribed for a variety of ailments, including gout, stomach, kidney, and liver issues. Today, they are mainly known for giving gin its distinctive flavor.

083

TAKE A TONIC

history

It's said that the primary tool that allowed England to colonize tropical locations wasn't its naval might but the humble gin and tonic. Ground Peruvian cinchona bark mixed with water delivered a dose of the antimalarial compound quinine, but the colonists needed a little motivation to down the sludgy, bitter drink, and adding gin was the answer. Even after more effective malaria treatments were developed, tonic water remained popular. A more refreshing and less quinine-saturated version could be appreciated as a flavor element rather than as a treatment.

084

KNOW YOUR GINS

Gin comes in a number of styles. Here are the ones you're most likely to encounter.

GENEVER Said to be the original style of gin first produced by the Dutch, genever is made of and sweetened slightly with a malt wine base, lending it a flavor something like a cross between whiskey and beer. The Dutch tradition is to consume it from a *koopstojie*, which translates into "headbutt," a small, tulip-shaped glass filled so full that moving it will spill the contents. To drink, you must bow your head to the bar (almost like a headbutt) in order to slurp off enough that you can raise the glass and drink the rest.

LONDON DRY The most common style, London Dry is probably what you think of when you think of gin (that is, if you don't think about that horrible morning in college after drinking gin all night). Clean and unsweetened, the dry spirit can range from vegetal to spiced or floral, but it is always juniper-centric. Despite the fact that you can make it anywhere in the world—not just in London—it is the most versatile of the gin family. Oddly, it is rarely drunk alone as a shot.

OLD TOM This particular variation of gin is slightly drier than genever but slightly sweeter than London Dry gin.

SLOE GIN Sloe gin is really a liqueur, but it's made with gin steeped with sloe berries. These berries are related to plums; in Europe, the thorny shrubs were often used to create cattle-proof barriers. After flavoring the gin, the tart and slightly bitter berries are removed and sweetened. It can be enjoyed alone as an after-dinner cordial or more typically in a Sloe Gin Fizz.

MODERN During the recent craft cocktail boom, a new, less juniper-centric style of gin appeared on the scene. Focused more on spices, citrus, or herbs, this modern style lies somewhere on the spectrum between flavored vodka and London Dry. The flavor profile can be all over the place, but most of these gins are designed to work well either paired with tonic or used in a martini.

085

MIX IT OLD SCHOOL

Think of the Old Fashioned as the Mr. Potato Head of cocktails. It is one of the oldest and simplest drinks, not requiring anything beyond a glass, some booze, sweetener, and bitters. The recipe is more template than temple, allowing for substitutions for any of its components. You want to put its ear where its eye usually goes? It won't care, and it's possibly be more fun that way.

1 sugar cube (or ¾ teaspoon granulated sugar or 1 teaspoon rich simple syrup)

2 dashes of bitters (usually Angostura)

A few dashes of water

2 oz whiskey

Lemon peel

•➔ *Add the sugar to an old-fashioned or rocks glass, then add bitters and enough water to moisten the sugar. Using a muddler, crush the sugar, dissolving as much as possible. Add a large cube of ice and the whiskey, giving it a stir with a barspoon. Express the lemon peel over the drink and then drop it in the glass.*

086 { THE MUDDLED OLD FASHIONED }

Before the craft cocktail revival inspired bartenders to explore the historic recipes of the past, this style of Old Fashioned, with orange and cherry, was the standard recipe. In many bars, it still is.

1 cube sugar (about ¾ of a teaspoon)

Soda water

2 dashes bitters (typically Angostura)

2 orange slices

2 cocktail cherries

2 oz rye or bourbon whiskey

Add the sugar to an old-fashioned glass, then moisten it by adding bitters and just enough soda water to soak the sugar. Add 1 orange slice and 1 cherry to the glass. Using a muddler, crush the lot until the sugar dissolves. Using tongs or a barspoon, remove the orange rind, then add a large cube of ice and the whiskey, giving it a stir with a barspoon. Top with a splash of soda water, and garnish with the remaining orange and cherry speared with a cocktail pick.

USBG | SAN FRANCISCO CHAPTER

✦ KEVIN DIEDRICH ✦

Operating Manager | Pacific Cocktail Haven

087

THE KENTUCKY CONNECTION

Kevin Diedrich created a house Old Fashioned by using small tweaks on flavor to make a big impact. His version blends brandy and whiskey plus three different bitters. Start with 1 ounce each of cognac and whiskey, add 1 teaspoon demerara rich simple syrup (2:1), 2 dashes of Angostura bitters, and 2 dashes of citrus bitters (orange bitters mixed with lemon bitters at 2:1). Stir with ice and garnish with orange and lemon twists. The cognac complements the bourbon's citrus notes, and the bourbon's oak flavors bring out fruitcake notes in the cognac.

088 THE WISCONSIN OLD FASHIONED

The state drink of Wisconsin, where the Old Fashioned never dies, this regional variation can come four different ways: topped with sweet (lemon-lime soda), sour (sour mix or grapefruit soda), seltzer, or press (a mix of lemon-lime soda and seltzer). Garnishes can also range from the ubiquitous orange and cherry to pickled veggies.

1 sugar cube
(about ¾ of a teaspoon)

2 dashes bitters (typically Angostura)

Soda water, sour mix, lemon-lime or grapefruit

2 orange slices

2 cocktail cherries

2 oz California brandy (Korbel is standard in Wisconsin) or cognac

Add the sugar to an old-fashioned glass, then add bitters and enough seltzer or soda to soak the sugar. Add 1 orange slice and 1 cherry. Using a muddler, crush the lot until the sugar dissolves. Add the brandy, give it a quick stir, then add a large cube of ice. Top with a splash of your choice, and garnish with the remaining orange and cherry speared with a cocktail pick.

089 { MANHATTAN }

The origins of the Manhattan cocktail are disputed, but the drink was developed sometime in the 1860s. Originally made with rye whiskey (our preferred way), it is often also made with bourbon and Canadian whisky. During prohibition, Canadian whisky was the bootleg spirit of choice, a custom that continued long after the country went dry.

2 oz rye whiskey

1 oz Italian (sweet) vermouth

2 dashes Angostura bitters

Cherries to garnish

Combine all ingredients except garnish in an ice-filled mixing glass and stir 20–30 seconds, until well chilled. Strain the cocktail into a chilled coupe or cocktail glass. Garnish with cherries pieced together with a cocktail pick.

090  MAKE IT PERFECT

 Mixing equal parts sweet and dry vermouth in a Manhattan makes it a Perfect Manhattan—perfect being the term used for recipes that include both kinds of vermouth. While "perfect" may be a totally subjective adjective, mixing sweet and dry vermouth does tilt the drink into a more herbal and spice-driven direction, sometimes even making the drink a little savory (depending on the vermouth). Try a lemon twist in place of the cherry when going for perfect.

USBG | SAN FRANCISCO CHAPTER

✦ **H. JOSEPH EHRMANN** ✦

Owner/Operator | Elixir Saloon

091

THE BOOTHBY

This version of William "Cocktail Bill" Boothby's signature cocktail comes from barman H. Joseph Ehrmann. Boothby was a bartender and author who tended bar at the Palace Hotel in San Francisco in the pre-quake days of the early 1900s. This variation on a Manhattan strikes the right sweetness and bitter balance, and it lends a nice effervescence and sophistication worthy of a cocktail party.

1½ oz bonded rye whiskey

1½ oz Italian (sweet) vermouth

2 dashes Angostura bitters

1 oz sparkling wine (Brut preferred)

Combine all ingredients except sparkling wine in an ice-filled mixing glass and stir 20–30 seconds, until well chilled. Strain the cocktail into a chilled coupe or cocktail glass. Float sparkling wine on top.

092 { WORK YOUR CANADIAN WHISKY }

→ Of all the whiskies, the Canadian varieties are perhaps the most complicated to grasp, as all Canadian whisky gets lumped into one huge category, from the lowest-end blended stuff with added juices and sweeteners to the artisanal single-grain whiskies. Add to the confusion the popular belief that Canadian is a rye whisky (some are, but not all make whisky with rye in it). It's simplest to remember that, much like Scotch, Canadian whisky boasts a wide range of flavors.

What makes Canadian whisky unique is how it's made: Each type of grain used (which varies from distiller to distiller) is fermented and distilled separately, not mixed together as with bourbon. In the case where a blended whisky is being made, two different kinds of distillate are produced: one to a high proof and a second "flavoring" whisky distilled to a lower proof. They are both aged, with each type of grain kept in separate casks until it's time to bottle.

093 | MAKE IT A SNOW DAY

Sure, a warm drink on a cold day can be nice, but why not embrace nature and use the gifts of the season to chill your favorite beverage? People all over the world have been mixing delicious flavors with fresh-fallen snow since time immemorial, and modern bartenders are getting in on the fun. There are endless ways to experiment, but here are three methods to get you started.

CHILL IT You'd rather have a strong, cold, undiluted drink? Partially bury your bottle, glass, or flask in the snow and wait a few minutes. (It doesn't have to be complicated to be good.)

SHAKE IT Use clean, new snow in place of crushed ice in your shaker and shake gently. Snow texture varies, but even the iciest stuff is more delicate than crushed ice and will dissolve more quickly, adding dilution. If you want to minimize this effect, start with chilled ingredients and roll rather than shake.

SLUSH IT Think of this as a grown-up snow cone or slushie. Lightly pack some fresh-fallen snow into an already-chilled glass. Mix the non-booze ingredients for your favorite cocktail, and gently pour over the snow. Finally, swirl the booze on top and serve with a spoon. (If your favorite drink requires muddling, do the muddling at the very bottom, before adding the snow.)

094

ROB ROY

A variation of a Manhattan cocktail, the Rob Roy is thought to have originated in 1894 at New York's Waldorf Astoria hotel for the premiere of an operetta about the life of the Rob Roy MacGregor, known as the Scottish Robin Hood.

2 oz blended Scotch whisky

1 oz sweet vermouth

2 dashes Angostura or other aromatic bitters

Cherries to garnish

Combine all ingredients except garnish in an ice-filled mixing glass and stir 20–30 seconds, until well chilled. Strain the cocktail into a chilled coupe or cocktail glass. Garnish with cherries pieced together with a cocktail pick.

095

MAKE IT BURNS

The Bobby Burns cocktail is a simple variation of the Rob Roy that shows up with either the addition of ¼ ounce of herbal Benedictine or ½ teaspoon of absinthe. Each one a little different: The Benedictine version is dark and chocolatey, while the absinthe one is lighter and brighter.

096 | STUDY YOUR SCOTCH WHISKY

Like Ireland, Scotland has had some form of whisky distilled on its soil since around the 11th century, more or less. The cold weather and common practice of aging in used oak barrels makes for Scotch that can sit in its cask for a significant amount of time. While blended whisky makes up the bulk of its exports, the demand for malt whiskies (with unique regional differences) has put a strain on older stocks. Few forecasters predicted the sudden uptick in demand for Scotch, and so distilleries have had no choice but to increasingly release malt whiskies with no age statement—at least until supply meets demand in a decade or two. Here are the types to know.

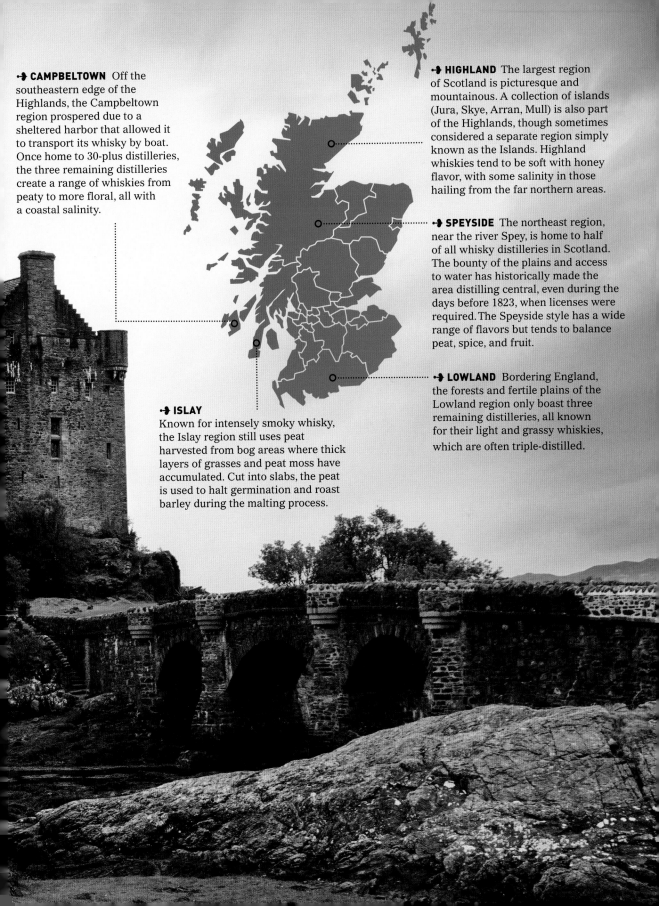

↦ CAMPBELTOWN Off the southeastern edge of the Highlands, the Campbeltown region prospered due to a sheltered harbor that allowed it to transport its whisky by boat. Once home to 30-plus distilleries, the three remaining distilleries create a range of whiskies from peaty to more floral, all with a coastal salinity.

↦ HIGHLAND The largest region of Scotland is picturesque and mountainous. A collection of islands (Jura, Skye, Arran, Mull) is also part of the Highlands, though sometimes considered a separate region simply known as the Islands. Highland whiskies tend to be soft with honey flavor, with some salinity in those hailing from the far northern areas.

↦ SPEYSIDE The northeast region, near the river Spey, is home to half of all whisky distilleries in Scotland. The bounty of the plains and access to water has historically made the area distilling central, even during the days before 1823, when licenses were required. The Speyside style has a wide range of flavors but tends to balance peat, spice, and fruit.

↦ LOWLAND Bordering England, the forests and fertile plains of the Lowland region only boast three remaining distilleries, all known for their light and grassy whiskies, which are often triple-distilled.

↦ ISLAY Known for intensely smoky whisky, the Islay region still uses peat harvested from bog areas where thick layers of grasses and peat moss have accumulated. Cut into slabs, the peat is used to halt germination and roast barley during the malting process.

097

GET JAZZY WITH SAZERACS

The official cocktail of New Orleans, the Sazerac as we know it today is the result of an evolution that started at the Sazerac Coffee House in the Big Easy, where Sazerac-de-Forge et Fils cognac was being imported from France in the 1850s. Their cocktail was a simple variation of what was then called a bitter sling (and what we know as an Old Fashioned) made of brandy, sugar, water, absinthe, and bitters from an old family recipe by Antoine Amedie Peychaud. By the 1870s, the drink changed to a rye whiskey base, as the Great French Wine Blight withered the supplies of cognac. Here is a variation on the drink, and the classic.

✦ JASON FOUST ✦

USBG Midwestern Regional VP

098

CLASSIC SAZERAC

Jason Faust supplies us with the cocktail formula for a classic Sazarac. For an old-school twist, swap out the whiskey for cognac—you'll get a real taste of the 1850s.

1 demerara sugar cube

3 dashes Peychaud's bitters

Rye whiskey

¼ oz Herbsaint (or absinthe)

Lemon peel

•➡ *Fill an old-fashioned or rocks glass with ice and set aside. In a pint or mixing glass, add the sugar cube and soak it with Peychaud's bitters, then muddle. Add rye whiskey and ice, then stir until sugar is dissolved. Remove ice from the glass, pour in the Herbsaint or absinthe, and swirl to coat the glass. Strain the cocktail from the mixing or pint glass into the prepared glass. Express lemon peel over drink and place in drink.*

MATT COWAN ✦ Cocktail Curator | La Cour

099 { POMME D'AMOUR }

A blend of the old and new versions of the Sazerac, this drink mixes whiskey with French brandy. The name translates into "toffee apple," and the flavors are perfect for the fall.

•➡ *Fill an old-fashioned or rocks glass with ice and set aside. In a pint or mixing glass, add the sugar cube and soak it with the bitters, then muddle. Add rye whiskey and Calvados, and stir until sugar dissolves. Add ice, then stir to chill the drink. Remove ice from the old-fashioned glass, pour in the absinthe, and swirl to coat the glass. Strain the cocktail from the mixing or pint glass into the prepared glass. Flame the lemon peel over the drink (see item 262) and place swath in the drink.*

1 demerara sugar cube

2 dashes Peychaud's bitters

2 dashes apple bitters

1 oz rye whiskey

1 oz Calvados apple brandy

Absinthe, to rinse glass

Lemon peel

100

TASTE THE MARTINI'S TIMELINE

Few cocktails can boast the kind of evolution that the martini has undergone—it's a drink that changes at the rate of fashion more than food. At the Interval Bar, bar director Jennifer Colliau tells the history of the drink through six different versions, covering some 250 years in the process. It's a story that not only encompasses the progress in cultural tastes but also shows how something can change and still maintain its identity.

101 J.P.A. MARTINI

When the German composer Johann Paul Aegidius Schwartzendorf moved to France in the late 1700s as a court musician, he changed his last name to Martini, as it was fashionable to have an Italian-sounding last name. He was known for drinking Dutch genever gin mixed with wine and ground cinnamon, a concoction that is believed to be the first Martini.

2 oz genever
(Diep9 preferred)

1 oz Chablis white wine

Cinnamon stick

Combine genever gin and Chablis in a pint or mixing glass, add ice, and stir 20–30 seconds until it reaches 32°F (0°C). Strain the cocktail into a Nick and Nora or small coupe or cocktail glass. Grate cinnamon over the glass.

102 { JULIA CHILD (AKA INVERTED MARTINI) }

Colliau provides this variation of the standard 2:1 gin to vermouth ratio, flipping the proportions to make the drink lighter and more vermouth-heavy—the way, it's said, Julia Child preferred it.

3¾ oz dry vermouth

¾ oz London Dry gin

Lemon peel

Combine all ingredients except lemon peel in a pint or mixing glass, add ice, and stir 20–30 seconds until it reaches 32°F (0°C). Strain the cocktail into a coupe or cocktail glass. Express lemon peel over drink and garnish with the peel.

103

MARTINEZ

The drink that is often credited as the ancestor of the martini has a hazy and conflicting history with lots of romantic stories—like the one about a miner on his way to Martinez.

2 oz Old Tom gin

1 oz Sweet vermouth (Dolin rouge preferred)

2 dashes orange bitters

Lemon peel

•♦ Combine all ingredients, except lemon peel, in a mixing glass, add ice, and stir 20–30 seconds until it reaches 32°F (0°C). Strain the cocktail into a Nick and Nora or coupe or cocktail glass. Express lemon peel over drink and garnish with the peel.

104

VESPER

You can't talk about the heritage of the martini without discussing the influence of Ian Fleming's James Bond. This variation was an invention of Fleming's, named for Bond's flame Vesper Lynd.

1½ oz London Dry gin

¾ oz vodka

½ oz Cocchi Americano aperitif wine

Lemon peel

•♦ Combine all ingredients, except lemon peel, in a cocktail shaker with ice. Shake hard 8–10 seconds and strain into a coupe or cocktail glass. Express lemon peel over drink and garnish with the peel.

✦ **JENNIFER COLLIAU** ✦

Owner of Small Hand Foods

105

DIRTY MARTINI

Based on a recipe of a dirty martini developed by Naren Young at Saxon + Parole in New York, this version shows that you can get dirty and stay classy.

1½ oz navy-strength gin

1½ oz dirty vermouth*

Olive

Extra-virgin olive oil

•➤ *To make the dirty vermouth, combine 375 ml dry vermouth, 4 oz pitted black Cerignola olives, and a pinch of salt in a blender; pulse until the olives are the texture of sand. Strain through a fine-mesh strainer and allow to stand until the fine olive pieces sink to the bottom. Strain again, carefully, leaving the sediment behind.*

•➤ *To mix your cocktail, combine gin and dirty vermouth in a pint or mixing glass, add ice, and stir 20–30 seconds until it reaches 32°F (0°C). Strain the cocktail into a coupe or cocktail glass. Garnish with an olive and a few drops of the olive oil.*

✦ **JENNIFER COLLIAU** ✦

Owner of Small Hand Foods

106

FIFTY-FIFTY SPLIT

A play on the 50-50 Martini by Audrey Saunders at her New York bar Pegu Club, which blended equal parts vermouth and gin, this version from beverage director of the Slanted Door Group Erik Adkins blends two different vermouths. It makes the drink at once more aromatic and drier.

1½ oz London Dry gin

¾ oz dry vermouth (Dolin preferred)

¾ oz blanc (or bianco) vermouth (Dolin preferred)

1 dash orange bitters

Lemon peel

•❥ *Combine all ingredients except lemon peel in a pint or mixing glass, add ice, and stir 20–30 seconds until it reaches 32°F (0°C). Strain the cocktail into a coupe or cocktail glass. Express lemon peel over drink and garnish with the peel.*

IAN ADAMS ✦ General Manager and Sherry Curator | 15 Romolo

107 { MAKE YOUR OWN VERMOUTH BASE }

If you start getting really into vermouth, you can mix yourself a custom batch. Try it a few times before tweaking the recipe, just so you get a sense of the baseline formula—this recipe contains all the botanicals you need to mix up a batch of either a bianco or a rosso sherry-based vermouth.

1.5 g wormwood

1.5 g elecampane

0.3 g angelica root

3 vanilla beans

5 g bitter orange peel

1.125 g Herbs de Provence

0.6 g coriander seed

0.5 g nutmeg, grated

0.7 g cinnamon stick

0.4 g chamomile

0.25 g damiana

0.4 g rooibos tea

Fresh zest of half an orange

375 ml VS Armagnac

375 ml pear liqueur (for bianco vermouth) OR

375 ml *patxaran* (for rosso vermouth)

•❥ *Combine all ingredients together and allow to macerate, covered, for 48 hours in a cool, dark space. Once the infusion is complete, strain and proceed to the final mixing steps.*

•❥ *For bianco, combine 375 ml of your vermouth base with 1.1125 ml fino sherry (a 750 ml bottle plus a 375 ml bottle). Allow ingredients to marry overnight; then mix away!*

•❥ *For rosso, combine 375 ml vermouth base with 1.1125 ml cream sherry (again, that's one 750 ml bottle plus one 375 ml bottle). Allow ingredients to marry overnight; then mix away!*

✦ JASON FOUST ✦

USBG Midwestern Regional VP

108

SONG ABOUT AN EX

Inspired by a visit to Copper & Kings distillery in Kentucky, where each still is named after a Bob Dylan song and music is played in the barrel-aging warehouse to agitate the brandy, barman Jason Faust developed this cocktail that blends American, Italian, and French to toast an old flame.

1½ oz aged brandy (Copper & Kings preferred)

¾ oz Yellow Chartreuse

¾ oz Cynar

2 dashes grapefruit bitters

Lemon peel

Combine all ingredients except lemon peel in a mixing glass, add ice, and stir 20–30 seconds. Strain the cocktail into a brandy snifter or rocks (or old-fashioned) glass. Express lemon peel over drink and garnish with peel in drink.

JEFF LYON ✦ Owner/Operator | Third Rail

109  BONE MACHINE

No, this drink is not named after a wrestler, a porn actor, or a Pixies album—but it is named after a 1992 Grammy-winning Tom Waits album. This cocktail is designed to showcase sherry as a cocktail ingredient—which may sound feisty, but it turns out dry and easy-drinking, with lots of citrus brightness.

1½ oz Oloroso sherry

1 oz bourbon whiskey

1 oz Amaro Nonino

1 oz Benedictine liqueur

1 dash Aromatic bitters

2 dashes orange bitters

Orange peel

Combine all ingredients except orange peel in a mixing glass, add ice, and stir 20–30 seconds. Strain the cocktail into an old-fashioned or rocks glass with one large ice cube. Flame orange peel over drink (see item 262) and garnish with peel in drink.

CHRISTOPHER DAY ✦ Bar Manager | General Lee's Cocktail House

110 BENDING BLADES

The Blades is a tequila martini for the summertime, with lots of juicy, refreshing flavors that finish nice and dry. It's like sitting under the shade surrounded by the smell of freshly-cut grass.

½ oz blanco tequila

½ oz grapefruit liqueur (Giffard Pamplemousse Rose preferred)

½ oz Manzanilla sherry (Lustau Papirusa preferred)

½ oz Salers Aperitif gentian liqueur

Lemon peel

Combine all ingredients except lemon peel in a mixing glass, add ice, and stir 20–30 seconds. Strain the cocktail into a Nick and Nora or small coupe or cocktail glass. Express lemon peel over drink and discard peel.

USBG | DENVER CHAPTER

✦ ANDREAS PEJOVIC ✦

Bartender | OAK at fourteenth

111

BROKEN COMPASS

Inspired by the story of a Norwegian ship that loses its way, this drink tells the tale (in liquid form) of a broken compass and a crew's stops in Jamaica, Curaçao, and Spain on the way back home.

¾ oz navy-strength Jamaican rum

¾ oz Aquavit (Linie, which is aged in used Oloroso sherry casks preferred)

¾ oz Manzanilla sherry

½ oz curaçao (Pierre Ferrand Dry Curaçao preferred)

¼ oz grenadine

1 dash almond extract

Orange peel, cut into the shape of a compass arrow

•➔ *Combine all ingredients except orange peel in a mixing glass, add ice, and stir 20–30 seconds. Strain the cocktail into an old-fashioned or rocks glass with one large ice cube. Express orange peel over drink and garnish with peel on top of ice.*

RUM

PART OF THE REASON RUM BECAME SUCH A HUGE COMMODITY IN THE 17TH CENTURY WAS THE FACT THAT IT WAS MADE FROM WHAT WAS CONSIDERED WASTE PRODUCT FROM SUGAR PRODUCTION.

112

LEARN THE HISTORY

➤ Every 100 tons of sugarcane yields 10 tons of refined sugar, plus 5 tons of "waste" in the form of molasses. And every ton of molasses yields approximately 70 gallons (265 l) of rum. That's a lot of mai tais.

The flip side of rum's success is much bleaker, in the slave trafficking that took place as part of the Trade Triangle. Molasses was brought to the American colonies, where it was distilled into rum, which was then traded in Africa for slaves, who were brought to the Caribbean to work in the sugarcane plantations. This continued until the early 19th century.

When a British blockade cut off France's access to their Caribbean colonies, Napoleon banned the importation of sugar into France, kicking off the beet sugar industry. When France no longer depended on cane for sugar, the refineries were left in near financial collapse. The islands soon began to produce rum from the fresh cane juice rather than bothering to refine the sugar, leading to an entirely new style of rum.

Central and South America also got in on the rum action when the Portuguese and Spanish brought in sugarcane. Brazil became (and remains) one of the world's biggest sugar producers. Meanwhile, Facundo Bacardi Massó, a Spanish wine merchant, used a column still and charcoal filtration to produce a smoother rum—a style so popular that it spread to other colonies.

113

DRINK IN TONGUES
geography

The type of rum produced in the Caribbean, as well as Central and South America, can be distinguished in style by the primary language spoken. In English-speaking countries, the rum will be dark and flavorful, with Jamaican rums being the most robust. Spanish-speaking countries will favor cleaner-tasting rums aged in barrels, while French-speaking countries make rum from fresh cane juice instead of molasses—creating something brawny and funky, with a lot of flavor, though lighter than Jamaican rum.

Making rum always begins with some form of sugarcane, and while molasses is most common, any form can be used, from fresh cane juice to all forms of granulated cane sugar.

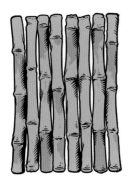  

•➧ STEP ONE The cane sugar is diluted with water, allowing yeast to ferment the sucrose. Some distilleries let wild yeasts to do the work, others use custom strains, and another set, such as those in Jamaica, adds dunder (the foam from previous fermentations).

•➧ STEP TWO Depending on the ambient heat, the ferment could be ready as soon as 24 hours later, although some distilleries cool the fermentation tanks, slowing the process to allow for increased flavor production from the yeast.

•➧ STEP THREE The ferment is double distilled, either in pot stills (for richer flavors) or by running through a continuous still (for cleaner flavors).

•➧ STEP FOUR The rum is most often aged in wood, or, at the very least, rested in stainless-steel tanks before bottling.

115

TICK OFF THE TYPES

It's worth knowing the difference between the various types of rum—there may be more than you think, and the flavor of your cocktail hangs in the balance.

 LIGHT RUM Clear rum, typically made of molasses and distilled to a high proof for a very clean flavor, is known as light rum. Additionally, aged rums stripped of their color through filtering are sometimes added to increase depth of flavor. Light rum is the type most often used in cocktails.

 GOLDEN/AGED RUM Mellow and easy-drinking, golden or aged rum is molasses-based and gets its distinctive color from barrel aging (sometimes also augmented with caramel). It makes for a good digestive after a nice meal.

 DARK/JAMAICAN RUM Molasses-based rums aged for a long time and with much of the molasses flavors left intact during distillation are known as dark or Jamaican rums. They are very full-flavored, with a heft that makes them useful in mixed drinks, such as the classic Mai Tai (see item 149).

 RHUM AGRICOLE Pot-distilled and often left alone to naturally ferment, rhum agricole can be vegetal, rustic, and funky in its unaged form—characteristics that are tamed a little as it ages in the barrel. Think of it this way: rhum agricole is to rum what peaty Scotch is to blended whisky.

 CACHAÇA Brazil is the biggest grower of sugarcane, and it's the country that also produces cachaça, a spirit distinguished from rum in that it is made from fresh cane juice instead of sugar byproducts. While most of the exported cachaça is unaged and distilled through column stills to produce a grassy but clean liquor, cachaça can also be made in pot stills and aged like other sugarcane-based spirits. These cachaças are aged in oak or other more exotic woods like Brazilian jequitiba rosa or balsam of Tolu.

FLAVORED RUMS Until the last couple of years, flavored rums were primarily artificially flavored (despite the "natural flavors" claims often found on the labels). Now, however, there are many alternatives, including versions created by infusing and distilling actual fruit. They are worth seeking out, especially the pineapple and coconut versions—they taste like warm Caribbean water lapping over your bare feet in the soft sand.

For beginners, it can be helpful to start with a glass and tin version, as building the drink in the glass will allow you to see exactly what's happening, especially when muddling. The two-tin style is much lighter, which can be helpful for maintaining your stamina when shaking a lot of cocktails.

BOSTON OR TWO-PART SHAKER The workhorse of the bar is this style of shaker that consists of two pieces: a metal tin and a smaller tin or tempered glass cup that fits inside the larger tin.

116 | GET TO KNOW THE MOVERS AND SHAKERS

One of the key pieces of equipment (and perhaps the one most closely associated with cocktail making by the general public) is the shaker. Shakers are primarily used for mixing drinks containing juice, dairy, or eggs—in order to quickly cool down the ingredients—but also to develop texture. There are no hard and fast rules about what shaker you should use, and, like any tool, there's a time and place for all of them. Strainers also come in more varieties than you might think for a simple bar tool.

COBBLER OR THREE-PART SHAKER The most iconic model, the cobbler shaker comes in three parts: a large base for the ice and ingredients, a top with a built-in strainer, and a cap. While great for making a single drink, problems can arise when there's a crowd. The cold tin can cause ice to form at the seams, freezing the pieces shut and making opening the shaker frustrating enough to drive you to drink unmixed cocktails.

FRENCH OR PARISIAN SHAKER Another two-part mixing tin that looks like a cross between a cobbler and Boston shaker, the French-style shaker has a cap with curvy shoulders, which provides a nice grip. What it lacks in versatility it makes up for in elegance.

117

OPEN THE FLOODGATES

At first, getting your perfectly mixed cocktail out of the shaker can feel harder than making it, but here are a few secrets to busting your cocktail out.

For a cobbler shaker, get a towel wet with warm water and place it on the cap (only on the cap or you'll warm up your drink) for a minute. Twist the cap back and forth until it comes free.

If you're using a Boston shaker with a glass tumbler, hold the metal part of the shaker with your nondominant hand and give the area where the seal is flush a pop with the heel of your other hand.

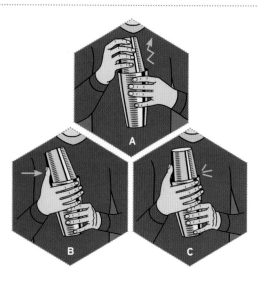

If you've gone all metal with a small and big tin, hold the bigger tin in your nondominant hand and give it a squeeze while you move the smaller tin back and

forth (A). It should come free, but if it doesn't, hold the larger tin firmly (B) and use your thumb to push the smaller tin on the flush side toward the other end (C).

118 DON'T STRAIN YOURSELF

Strainers also come in more varieties than you might think for a simple bar tool. Each has its own set of strengths and weaknesses, and each can be best suited for certain types of cocktails. As always, find what works for you and make the most of it.

FINE STRAINER These small mesh strainers are necessary for shaken drinks where texture is key—as is keeping ice chips or muddled ingredients out of the drink.

JULEP STRAINER Looking like an oversize slotted spoon, the julep strainer is used for stirred drinks, since it only needs to keep large chucks of ice out.

HAWTHORNE STRAINER The more versatile of the two, the Hawthorne's spring allows it to fit most tins and glasses, and can be used for both shaken and stirred drinks.

✦ MARCOS TELLO ✦

Bar & Spirits Consultant

119 | UNDERSTAND THE SHAKE

➤→ The best part of making cocktails is shaking them—there's something immensely satisfying about the sound of rattling ice inside the tins. And how you shake your drinks will have an impact on what ends up in the cocktail glass.

UNDERSTAND THE MECHANICS The cooling action of a shake is much like that of a piston—as you move the shaker back and forth, the ice and liquid collide into each other, chilling and aerating the cocktail. You can tell how cold your drink is by how cold the tin is, but at least 8–10 seconds of shaking is ideal.

KNOW SIZE MATTERS With most cocktails, standard-size ice works perfectly well, but if you want to get geeky, you can fine-tune the drink by changing the size of the ice. Using a single large cube will increase aeration and texture, while shaking a drink with crushed ice will increase dilution.

SHAKE YOUR HEART OUT Shaking the drink is part of the entertainment aspect of bartending, so think of it as a performance. Add some dance moves and make it fun. There is nothing sadder (or less cold) than a half-hearted shake.

DON'T GET HURT Repetitive stress injuries are a real danger of bartending, and rhythm and bounce are important to avoid injury. Keep a tight core, think of sinking your shoulder blades into your back pockets, and let the power come from your legs, like a boxer.

120 | SHAKE YOUR COCKTAIL MAKER

There are a few key steps to follow when shaking a drink in order to keep the process streamlined—and to make sure your drink stays inside the shaker.

⟶ STEP ONE Build the drink by starting with juices and syrups first, then adding the liquor at the end. This allows you to start over in case you make a mistake—without having to dump out excess booze.

⟶ STEP TWO Once the liquid components are in the glass, then add the ice. This allows for interruptions or distractions without worrying about the cocktail over-diluting while you tend to other matters.

⟶ STEP THREE Place the larger mixing tin on top of the glass or smaller tin, giving it a quick tap with the palm of your hand to secure it. Alternatively, if you are building multiple drinks in the larger tin, secure the smaller tin or glass with the same tap. You want to make sure you have a tight seal—or people in the first two rows may get wet.

⟶ STEP FOUR Grip the large tin with both hands, and shake with the seal and glass facing you. This ensures that if the seal accidentally breaks, no one but you and your bar back will notice. If you get sprayed, tap the glass and try again.

⟶ STEP FIVE Shake the cocktail thoroughly and with some enthusiasm for about 10 seconds. You will feel the shaker get colder (and your cocktail get more delicious). To get the thing open again, see item 117.

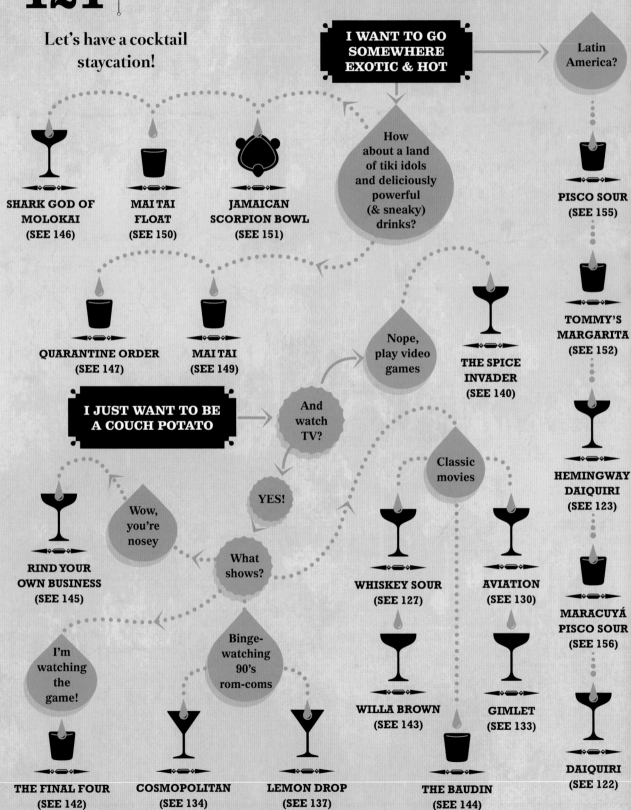

121 CHOOSE YOUR TART & TANGY DRINK

Let's have a cocktail staycation!

I WANT TO GO SOMEWHERE EXOTIC & HOT

Latin America?

How about a land of tiki idols and deliciously powerful (& sneaky) drinks?

SHARK GOD OF MOLOKAI (SEE 146)

MAI TAI FLOAT (SEE 150)

JAMAICAN SCORPION BOWL (SEE 151)

PISCO SOUR (SEE 155)

QUARANTINE ORDER (SEE 147)

MAI TAI (SEE 149)

Nope, play video games

THE SPICE INVADER (SEE 140)

TOMMY'S MARGARITA (SEE 152)

I JUST WANT TO BE A COUCH POTATO

And watch TV?

Classic movies

HEMINGWAY DAIQUIRI (SEE 123)

Wow, you're nosey

YES!

WHISKEY SOUR (SEE 127)

AVIATION (SEE 130)

RIND YOUR OWN BUSINESS (SEE 145)

What shows?

MARACUYÁ PISCO SOUR (SEE 156)

I'm watching the game!

Binge-watching 90's rom-coms

WILLA BROWN (SEE 143)

GIMLET (SEE 133)

THE FINAL FOUR (SEE 142)

COSMOPOLITAN (SEE 134)

LEMON DROP (SEE 137)

THE BAUDIN (SEE 144)

DAIQUIRI (SEE 122)

122

GET THE BASIC DAIQUIRI

Of all the cocktail families, the sours are probably the best known, with iconic, popular drinks like margaritas and daiquiris. The daiquiri is named for a mine in the Cuban city of Santiago de Cuba. The drink became popular after the recipe was introduced in 1909 to the Army and Navy Club in Washington, D.C., by Rear Admiral Lucius W. Johnson. Here's how to make the ultimate classic.

2 oz white rum

½ oz lime juice

½ oz simple syrup (1:1)

Lime wheel to garnish

•➜ *Combine all ingredients except garnish in a shaker. Add ice, shake hard 8–10 seconds, and strain into a cold coupe or cocktail glass. Garnish with a lime wheel.*

123

COMPOSE A HEMINGWAY DAIQUIRI

This variation is one that Hemingway supposedly drank—and he drank a lot of them.

2 oz white rum (aged rum will affect the color)

¾ oz lime juice

½ oz grapefruit juice

½ oz Maraschino liqueur (made from tart marasca cherries, which have an earthy, herbal, almond flavor)

Lime wheel to garnish

•➜ *Combine all ingredients except garnish in a shaker. Add ice, shake hard 8–10 seconds, and strain into a cold coupe or cocktail glass. Garnish with the lime wheel.*

124 MAKE IT FROZEN

Sometimes you need a little bit of the trashiness that comes with a frozen daiquiri. Luckily, you can make a classy (and delicious) version of the slushie machine favorite at home.

2 oz white rum (aged rum can be used, but it will affect the color)

¾ oz lime juice

1 oz simple syrup (1:1)

½ heaping cup crushed ice (or 4–5 regular ice cubes)

Lime wheel to garnish

•➜ *Combine all ingredients except garnish in a blender. Add ice and blend until the texture is creamy and the ice is uniformly crushed. Strain into a cold coupe or cocktail glass and garnish with the lime wheel.*

125 | RECRUIT SOME FRUIT

⊱→ Oh, you wanted a fruit-flavored, resort-vacation, cruise-ship daiquiri, not just the classic blended up?

Here's a version that gets a boost of flavor from fruit liqueur and works best with a corresponding frozen fruit (such as peach liqueur with frozen peaches, banana liqueur with frozen bananas, you get the idea).

If you don't want to do that— out of laziness or because you think you don't deserve such opulence (you do!)—you can substitute triple sec or just add more simple syrup.

2 oz white rum (aged rum can be used, but it will affect the color)

¼ cup chopped fruit (frozen)

1 oz lime juice

½ oz fruit liqueur

¾ oz simple syrup (1:1)

½ heaping cup crushed ice (or 4-5 regular ice-cube-tray ice cubes)

Lime wheel to garnish

•→ *Combine all ingredients in a blender. Add ice and blend until the texture gets creamy and the ice is uniformly crushed. Strain into a cold coupe or cocktail glass. Garnish with the lime wheel.*

126

KNOW YOUR AMERICAN WHISKEY

The arrival of the Scots and Irish in the 17th century marked the beginning of whiskey distilling in the United States, although it was all rye whisky until the late 1700s, when settlers reached the plains of Kentucky and Tennessee. Corn grew in abundance, and the recipe shifted to the more corn-dominant profile we know today.

BOURBON While it's commonly thought that bourbon whiskey is named after a county, which in turn was named after members of the French Royalty that aided the early colonists, it may in fact have been named after none other than the most famous Bourbon of them all: the street in New Orleans. The story goes that Kentucky whiskey was being placed into charred barrels to give the whiskey a Cognac-like flavor (favored by the citizens of New Orleans), and then shipped down the Ohio River. It's thought that people began to ask for it as the style sold on Bourbon Street. In order to be a bourbon whiskey, the liquor must meet the following criteria: It must be made in the continental United States; contain at least 51 percent corn; be aged for at least two years in brand-new, charred American Oak barrels; and be distilled no higher than 80 percent alcohol. Those standards allow for plenty of variation, including the ratios of corn to other grains, like rye and wheat.

TENNESSEE The key differences between bourbon and Tennessee whiskey come to two factors: Tennessee whiskey must be made in Tennessee, and filtered through maple charcoal—with one exception: Prichard's Tennessee Whiskey is exempt from the latter requirement. The owner of Prichard's objected on the basis that he didn't want to be required to make whiskey like Jack Daniel's.

RYE Much of the first whiskey distillation took place in Maryland and Pennsylvania with the grain that grew in abundance at the time: rye. The acclaim disappeared when Prohibition closed down production for good. Now most rye is made in many of the same distilleries and in the same way that bourbon is, with one key substitution: It must be made from at least 51 percent rye (instead of corn). Spicy and sometimes grassy or doughy, rye whiskey makes great stirred drinks like Manhattans (see item 089) and Old Pals (see item 061).

127 { CLASSIC WHISKEY SOUR }

This simple recipe does a great job of unpacking some of the different flavors and layers that the oak gives the whiskey. Cheap bourbon works well here, but a midrange whiskey will shine.

2 oz bourbon whiskey

1 oz lemon juice

½ oz simple syrup (1:1)

Cherry and orange slice to garnish

Combine all ingredients, except for the garnish, in a cocktail shaker. Add ice, shake hard 8–10seconds, and strain into a cold coupe or cocktail glass. Garnish with a cherry and orange slice pieced together with a cocktail pick.

128

GUM THINGS UP

The classic whiskey sour is sometimes made with an egg white to give the drink some body and a foamy white crown, but we find it unnecessary. If you want to add a little more weight to the drink, use gum syrup (simple syrup thickened with gum arabic). It was a popular bar ingredient in the pre-Prohibition days and will add a little viscosity and velvety smoothness to your drink.

129   GET IN THE LIMELIGHT

I prefer to have my whiskey sours made with a bit of lime juice mixed in with the lemon, about 1 lime to every 2 lemons. It gives it a bright accent that doesn't dominate or get in the way of the whiskey.

130 { THE CLASSIC AVIATION }

This cocktail, first developed by Hugo Ensslin in the early 20th century, originally contained crème de violette, a bluish-purple violet liqueur, but for the most part the drink is often made without it. Use it if you can find some—it gives it a lovely color and floral aroma.

2 oz gin

½ oz lemon juice

½ oz maraschino

¼ oz crème de violette (optional)

Cherry to garnish

Combine all ingredients except garnish in a cocktail shaker. Add ice, shake hard 8–10 seconds, and strain into a cold coupe or cocktail glass. Garnish with a cherry dropped into the glass so it sits at the bottom.

131

KEEP IT CORDIAL

Like the flavor of lime cordial but want to make it yourself? All you need is some sugar, limes, and water.

Combine ½ cup each sugar and water in a saucepan and heat until it reaches a simmer and the sugar dissolves. Remove from heat and add the zest from 1 lime, cover, and allow to cool.

Once cool, add 4 ounces of lime juice to the saucepan, stir to combine, then strain. Use as you would lime cordial—or mix it with seltzer (1 part cordial to 3 parts water) to make an excellent sparkling limeade.

132 ❖ MAKE IT BLUE

If you really like the taste of the crème de violette, you can make a Blue Moon, which uses the violette liqueur as the sole sweetener. Substitute the violette for the maraschino liqueur, for a total of ½ ounce of the crème.

133

GIMLET

Some bartenders say that the proper way to make a gimlet is with lime cordial (like Rose's lime juice) and that making this drink with fresh lime juice is technically a Rickey. Lime juice advocates say that the drink with lime juice is the way the drink was intended to be made. If you want to find out for yourself, simply replace both the simple syrup and lime juice with ¾ ounces of lime cordial.

2 oz gin

½ oz lime juice

½ oz simple syrup (1:1)

Lime wheel to garnish

Combine all ingredients except garnish in a shaker. Add ice, shake, and strain into a cold coupe or cocktail glass. Garnish with the lime wheel.

134

COSMOPOLITAN

The origins of the ubiquitous cosmo are, like many things that occur in bars, hazy. Some claim the drink was invented in the 1970s in Cleveland—or South Beach or Minneapolis—as a variation of a kamikaze (a cosmopolitan without the cranberry juice). It's also entirely possible the origins of the drink come from the 1934 book *Pioneers of Mixing at Elite Bars* which includes a recipe utilizing gin instead of vodka and raspberry syrup in place of the cranberry juice.

2 oz vodka

¾ oz lime juice

¼ oz cranberry juice

½ oz orange liqueur or triple sec

Lime wheel to garnish

Combine all ingredients except garnish in a cocktail shaker. Add ice, shake hard 8–10 seconds ,and strain into a cold coupe or cocktail glass. Garnish with the lime wheel.

135

SWAP THE CRANBERRY

➤ Try pomegranate, cherry, or even apple juice in place of the cranberry to give the drink a twist.

136

VARY THE VODKA

➤ Citrus-flavored or homemade infused vodka works great in this recipe, but keep a bottle of plain vodka handy—flavored vodkas can be too intense and throw the cocktail off balance. If this happens, just substitute 1 ounce each of plain for flavored to mellow things out.

137 { LEMON DROP }

Created sometime in the 1970s by Norman Jay Hobday at his bar Henry Africa's in San Francisco, this citrus-focused drink also works well with Meyer lemons.

Lemon wedge and superfine sugar

2 oz vodka (citrus or plain)

¾ oz lemon juice

½ oz orange liqueur (or triple sec) or simple syrup (1:1)

Lemon peel or lemon wheel to garnish (optional)

•➤ *Place enough superfine (or baker's) sugar to create a thin layer on a small plate. Moisten the rim of the glass by running a lemon wedge around the lip, then dipping and twirling the glass to coat the edge. Set the glass aside.*

•➤ *Combine vodka, lemon juice, and liqueur in a shaker. Add ice, shake hard, and strain into a cold coupe or cocktail glass. Garnish with lemon.*

138

EXTRACT FLAVOR LIKE A PRO

Making tinctures (see item 035) gives you another tool to enhance drinks with layers of flavors you may not get any other way. Kaleena Goldsworthy of Flying Squirrel Bar loves getting creative with her tinctures, and here she offers a couple of great ways to get started making and using these concentrated bursts of flavor.

139 | CONTROL THE SPICE, CONTROL THE COCKTAIL

Chile pepper tinctures are a great way to add a spicy kick to a drink with a nice measure of control. Using an eye dropper is also important to give you some precision. This recipe for a Hot Pepper Tincture works great for Bloody Marys (see item 183) and even in cooking. Just make sure to wear gloves while working, and don't touch your eyes—or anything else you don't want to singe!

2 whole fresh chiles, such as Fresnos, sliced

½ fresh habanero chile (with the seeds)

½ dried chipotle

4 oz 151-proof vodka (or 2 oz each Everclear and standard 80-proof vodka)

•➔ *In a small jar, combine chiles with vodka, making sure the peppers are fully submerged (add more vodka if needed). Place in a cool, dark location, giving the jar a daily shake for a week. Then strain the solids and reserve the liquid. Taste to determine the heat (try a drop in 1 oz water if you're feeling timid). Now, go scorch some cocktails.*

140 { THE SPICE INVADER }

In this spicy drink, the lemon peel is key. It offers a nice, fresh citrus nose (which also helps keep the heat from the tincture at bay), while the ginger liqueur's sweetness and flavor melds nicely with the tequila and citrus tartness. The hot pepper tincture creeps in at the end, rounding out this refreshing cocktail with a solid hit of heat.

6 drops Hot Pepper Tincture (see item 139)

1½ oz blanco Tequila

½ oz ginger liqueur

¼ oz lemon juice

Lemon peel

•➔ *Take a coupe or cocktail glass and place 6 drops of the Hot Pepper Tincture along the sides of the glass. You can put 7 in if you're feeling bold. Set the glass aside.*

•➔ *Combine the tequila, liqueur, and lemon juice in a shaker. Add ice, shake hard 8–10 seconds, and strain into the glass. Pinch lemon peel to perfume it with citrus oils, then drop it in the drink.*

141   ORANGE YOU GLAD YOU MADE A TINCTURE?

One lucky fruit gets transformed four different ways to showcase the nuanced degrees of citrus flavors in Kaleena's Four Orange Tincture.

3 oranges, organic and unwaxed if available

5 oz 151-proof vodka (or 2½ oz each Everclear and standard 80-proof vodka)

•➜ *Peel one of the oranges with a vegetable peeler to remove as much zest as you can with as little pith as possible. Place the peels on a parchment-lined baking sheet and dry at the lowest temperature in your oven until stiff, about an hour or two.*

•➜ *Break the dried peels apart into a small mason jar, and add the fresh peels from half an orange (only peel half of it). Cut and chop the unpeeled half orange (peel, flesh, and all) and add to the mason jar.*

•➜ *Peel the zest off half of the last orange and bake on a sheet pan in the oven until dried out, then broil until the edges are burned. Keep a close eye on the peels, as they will burn very fast. Remove from the oven and let cool.*

•➜ *Tear or chop the burned peels into the mason jar. Add the vodka to cover. Place in a cool, dark location, giving the jar a daily shake for three weeks. Then strain the solids and reserve the liquid.*

142

THE FINAL FOUR

The Final Four is a nice, light, and barely sweetened drink built with layers of flavor from the four different aspects of orange extracted in the tincture. The burned orange gives the combination richness and depth.

1¼ oz vodka

¼ oz Four Orange Tincture (see item 141)

¼ oz Dolin Véritable Génépy des Alpes (an herbal vermouth)

Seltzer

Orange peel to garnish

•➜ *In a rocks or old-fashioned glass with ice, add the vodka, Four Orange tincture, and Génépy, then top with seltzer. Pinch orange peel (with the skin side facing the drink), then drop it in the drink to garnish.*

USBG | AUSTIN CHAPTER

✦ **PATRICK LUSSIER** ✦

Bartender

143

WILLA BROWN

This bourbon twist on a classic Aviation is named after the Kentucky-born aviator, lobbyist, teacher, and civil rights activist Willa Beatrice Brown.

1½ oz bourbon

¾ oz lemon juice

½ oz maraschino liqueur

¼ oz crème de violette

Lime wheel

➜ *Combine all ingredients except lime wheel in a cocktail shaker. Add ice, shake hard 8–10 seconds, and strain into a cold coupe or cocktail glass. Garnish with a lime wheel.*

✦ T. COLE NEWTON ✦

Owner/Head Bartender

Twelve Mile Limit

144

THE BAUDIN

Named after the New Orleans street (and not the sausage—that's a boudin) and pronounced *bow-din*, this kicky variation of a whiskey sour is spicy enough to add a hum to your tongue without scorching it. Try it if you're in the mood for a twist without going too far outside your usual whiskey wheelhouse.

1½ oz bourbon

½ oz lemon juice

¾ oz rich honey syrup (2:1)

1 dash Tabasco sauce

Lemon peel

•➤ *Combine all ingredients except lemon peel in a cocktail shaker. Add ice, shake hard 8–10 seconds, and strain into a rocks or old-fashioned glass with fresh ice. Pinch the lemon peel over the drink (to express the citrus oils) and then drop it in the glass.*

RYAN SHIPMAN ✦ Bar Manager

145 { RIND YOUR OWN BUSINESS }

Designed for a customer looking for a custom drink that's fruity and refreshing, this cocktail demonstrates how mixing vodka with gin can introduce subtle botanical flavors.

1 oz gin

1 oz vodka

¾ oz mixed lemon and lime juice

¼ oz simple syrup

2 dashes Angostura or aromatic bitters

3 dashes grapefruit bitters

Lemon peel

•➤ *Combine all ingredients except lemon peel in a cocktail shaker. Add ice, shake hard 8–10 seconds, and strain into a coupe or cocktail glass. Pinch the lemon peel over the drink (to express the citrus oils) and then drop it in the glass.*

✦ ANDREW DOLINSKY ✦

Bartender | Cleveland Heath

146

SHARK GOD OF MOLOKAI

A professor of Polynesian studies named this cocktail after the legend of the Shark God, who helped priest Kamalo avenge the deaths of his sons by the chief Kupa. The Shark God created a tempest that swept the chief into the sea, where he was devoured by the god. This whisky-based tiki cocktail swirls with a storm of flavors ranging from fruity to herbaceous, with the float of bitters representing the sea red with blood.

1½ oz bourbon

¾ oz Swedish punch

¼ oz absinthe

¾ oz lemon juice

1 oz pineapple juice

2 dashes Peychaud's
(or creole) bitters

Mint

•✦ *Combine all ingredients except bitters and mint in a shaker. Add ice, shake hard 8–10 seconds, and strain into a cold coupe or cocktail glass. Make a line with the bitters on the surface of the drink, and garnish with a mint leaf "shark fin."*

WILLIAM PRESTWOOD ✦ Bartender | Pagan Idol

147 { QUARANTINE ORDER }

While playing around with grapefruit and cinnamon flavors (made famous by tiki barman Don the Beachcomber), Prestwood noticed the strong cinnamon flavors in bitters and decided to combine them with some of his favorite rum for a bitters-heavy tropical drink.

½ oz passion fruit syrup

2¼ teaspoons demerara cinnamon syrup

1½ oz Denizen Merchant's Reserve rum (a blend of rums from Jamaica and Martinique)

½ oz Hamilton Demerara 86 rum

1 oz grapefruit juice

½ oz lime juice

7 dashes Angostura bitters

Lime wheel and cherry flag to garnish (see item 253)

Sprig of mint to garnish

•✦ *Make the passion fruit syrup by combining 9 ounces passion fruit purée, 1 ounce water, and 15 ounces sugar in a saucepan; heat until dissolved. Make the cinnamon syrup by combining 1 cup water, 1 cinnamon stick, and 1½ cups demerara sugar in a saucepan, then heat.*

•✦ *Combine all ingredients except garnishes in a cocktail shaker. Shake (without ice) or stir to combine, and pour into a glass with crushed ice. Garnish with lime-cherry flag and slap the mint before putting in the glass.*

148

GO TIKI

Polynesian drinking establishments tend to boast a certain ambiance. Bamboo floors and wooden masks abound. It's all part of the bar culture first established by Don the Beachcomber in the 1930s, and it will only add to your cocktail experience.

149

MAI TAI

The Mai Tai we know and love today was invented in Oakland, California, in 1944 (it's true; naysayers, begone!) by Trader Vic. The name comes from a Tahitian phrase, mai tai roa, which loosely translates to "out of this world." As the story goes, Trader Vic had some friends from Tahiti at his bar and named the drink after their reaction to the first sip.

1 oz Jamaican rum (like Appleton Estate 12 Year)

1 oz Denizen Merchant's Reserve rum

¾ oz lime juice

½ oz dry curaçao

½ oz orgeat almond syrup

¼ oz simple syrup (1 part water to 1½ parts sugar)

Mint sprig

Lime wheel

Combine all ingredients except mint and lime wheel in a cocktail shaker. Add ice, shake hard 8–10 seconds, and strain into a cold glass. Garnish with the lime wheel and mint sprig.

150 { MAI TAI FLOAT }

A riff on the Mai Tai, this version is served at Pagan Idol in San Francisco and is well worth the extra effort to make.

¼ oz Fassionola Gold

1½ oz Denizen Merchant's Reserve rum

½ oz Santa Teresa 1796

1 oz lime juice

¾ oz Combier (an aged, brandy-based citrus liqueur)

½ oz orgeat almond syrup

½ oz House Float (see note)

Healthy mint sprig

Fruit stick (two cherries and a pineapple chunk)

Paper umbrella

•➤ *To make the Fassionola Gold, combine 10 ounces tropical fruit purée and 15 ounces sugar in a saucepan, and heat until the sugar dissolves. Combine rum, Santa Teresa, lime juice, Combier, and orgeat in a cocktail shaker with crushed ice. Shake hard 8–10 seconds and pour the whole thing into a large rocks or old-fashioned glass. Add House Float on top. Garnish with fruit, mint, and umbrella.*

•➤ *Note: The House Float is basically everything the staff at Pagan Idol finds to be delicious mixed together: Demerara rum, Oloroso/Pedro X sherry, créme de cacao, amaro, orange oil, love, and magic.*

151

JAMAICAN SCORPION BOWL

The Scorpion is one of the few tropical cocktails with roots in the South Pacific. This riff on the classic, developed by the staff at Pagan Idol, gets a powerful boost of flavor from the Jamaican rum. Don't forget to share—this is a king-size drink meant for at least (at least!) two people!

1½ oz overproof white rum

1½ oz aged Jamaican rum

1 oz VS cognac

4 oz orange juice

2 oz lemon juice

1½ oz orgeat

1 teaspoon demerara cinnamon syrup (see item 147)

Cinnamon stick, to grate

Gardenia flower

•➤ *Combine all ingredients except the cinnamon stick and flower in a blender with crushed ice. Blend 5 seconds and pour into a scorpion bowl (wahine bowl) with a handful of ice cubes. Grate cinnamon over the bowl, garnish with gardenia, and serve with extra-long drinking straws.*

152

TOMMY'S MARGARITA

➤➤ While the exact origins of the margarita are highly disputed, the version made famous by Julio Bermejo more than 30 years ago at Tommy's Mexican Restaurant in San Francisco is definitely not up for debate. The drink is simple, designed so that the lime juice and agave sweetener can best showcase the qualities of the tequila. The recipe allows you to taste the nuances of the agave spirit, rather than covering up the flavor.

To make a good margarita, start with 100 percent agave tequila. When Bermejo developed the recipe, he got rid of the mass-market tequilas that are made with 51 percent agave and 49 percent other sugars (plus 100 percent chance of hangover in every bottle). The switch raised the restaurant's cost of making margaritas by 300 percent, and Bermejo credits the drink's success to the fact that he was working for his parents, who couldn't fire him. It was stupid and radical and crazy, but it makes for fantastic drinks.

Another important ingredient is the agave simple syrup, which evolved out of Bermejo's preference for simple syrup instead of triple sec. When agave sweeteners became available, it was a no-brainer.

A final tip for the perfect margarita is to squeeze the limes as you make the drinks, and not ahead of time. As Bermejo says, "Fresh is like pregnant—either you are or you aren't."

2 oz 100 percent agave tequila

1 oz lime juice, fresh squeezed

1 oz agave simple syrup (1:1)

Combine all ingredients in a cocktail shaker with crushed ice. Shake hard 8–10 seconds and pour into a large rocks or old-fashioned glass.

153

KNOW YOUR HIGHLANDS AND LOWLANDS

Traditionally, most people divide tequila stylistically into two styles: highland or lowland (valley). In broad terms, lowland-style tequilas tend to be earthier, more pungent, greener, and more vegetal when they're unaged. Lowland tequilas tend to get aged in newer barrels, conditions that lend the aged tequila a quality more like whiskies and cognacs, and more reminiscent of stone fruit. Highland tequilas are spicy and citrusy when they're young. They tend to be aged in more neutral barrels that have aged many generations of product, and those flavors develop into notes of cooked citrus and winter spice.

>→ The problem with this simple division of tequila types is that 70 percent of all agave (for all tequila) comes from the highlands, leading to a blurring of the lines in terms of style. Even how they're aged is more a distiller's preference rather than a hard and fast rule. If you took two tequilas from the same region and aged them for the same amount of time—but in different barrels (one neutral and the other newer)—the contrast would be huge. The oak influence is a stylistic decision. Neither style is better nor worse, neither style tastes better nor worse—it's all a matter of what the individual guest enjoys.

154

USE A BLENDER JAR

>→ If you make it to Tommy's for a margarita, you'll quickly notice something unique: rather than shaking the drinks in a Boston shaker, the staff mix and shake them in a blender jar. And no, they don't use the blender.

It's a practical evolution from a time when all margaritas were ordered blended, and so the blender jars were readily available. Bermejo says that no one comes in and orders just one margarita, so the blender jar allows them to mix two at a time—or a whole four-drink pitcher.

✦ ENRIQUE SANCHEZ ✦

Bar Director | Arguello Restaurant

155

PISCO SOUR

The origins of both pisco liquor and the pisco sour cocktail are hotly debated topics among the Chileans and Peruvians. While both may be right, we prefer this classic version from Peruvian barman Enrique Sanchez to the eggless Chilean version. Sanchez got his start bartending at family events and quickly went from making party batches to making several thousand a week working at La Mar's San Francisco branch.

3 oz Quebranta grape pisco

1 oz simple syrup (1:1)

1 oz Peruvian lime juice (or Mexican key limes)

1 oz egg white (1 large egg's worth)

Angostura bitters

•✦ *Combine all ingredients except bitters, and use either the reverse dry-shake or blender methods (see items 157 and 158). Dot the frothy top with the bitters to garnish.*

ENRIQUE SANCHEZ ✦ Bar Director | Arguello Restaurant

156 ◇ MARACUYÁ PISCO SOUR

The *maracuyá*, or passion fruit, grows plentifully in Peru, and adding this tangy fruit gives it amazing flavor without overpowering the floral Italian grape-based pisco.

2 ½ oz Italia grape pisco

¾ oz passion fruit purée

½ oz lime juice

1 oz simple syrup (1:1)

1 oz egg white (1 large egg's worth)

Peychaud's bitters

•✦ *Combine all ingredients except bitters, and use either the reverse dry-shake or blender methods (see items 157 and 158). Dot the frothy top with the bitters to garnish.*

MARCOS TELLO ✦ Bar & Spirits Consultant

157 ◇ SHAKE IT HIGH AND DRY

When working with cocktails that contain cream or eggs for texture, using a three-part "reverse dry-shake" technique developed by Greek barman Aristotelis Papadopoulos will create a frothy and silky texture. Shaking a drink with egg whites rips apart its proteins through stress, then mixes them with the liquid and air to create a rich texture.

•✦ *Combine all of your ingredients in a shaker without ice and dry-shake 10 seconds. Add ice and shake another 10 seconds. Strain the drink, dump the ice, and shake again 10 more seconds.*

•✦ *If you're making a sour, strain the drink into a glass. If you're making a fizz, use a fine strainer. Nice, tight bubbles will rise better when you add the soda water and give your fizz a perfect head.*

USBG | SAN FRANCISCO CHAPTER

✦ **ENRIQUE SANCHEZ** ✦

Bar Director | Arguello Restaurant

158

BLEND YOUR PISCO

➤➤ You can make your pisco sours in batches (small or large) by using your blender instead of shaking each drink. Simply combine all the ingredients except bitters in a blender with a few ice cubes and bend until frothy. Strain into an old-fashioned or rocks glass.

BITTER LIQUEURS

USING ALCOHOL WITH MEDICINAL HERBS, ROOTS, SPICES, AND OTHER BOTANICALS TO CREATE A THERAPEUTIC TONIC DATES BACK TO THE FOURTH CENTURY B.C. WITH HIPPOCRATES, WHO WAS KNOWN TO CONCOCT WINE AND HERBAL REMEDIES TO BALANCE THE HUMORS AND THE BODY.

159

DRINK YOUR MEDICINE

➤ This practice of making a Hippocratic wine was an idea that carried through with the development of distillation. When the process was first discovered, much of what was being distilled was first and foremost considered pharmaceuticals.

Fundamentally, bitter liqueurs (*amaro* in Italian or *amer* in French) are based on the curative properties of a whole host of bitter barks, herbs, and roots. Most often, bitters include gentian (for its supposed fever reduction and other benefits) and cinchona (for its antimalarial and other uses),

frequently accompanied by orange peel for flavoring. On the herb side, wormwood (believed to have anti-parasitic properties) is used, as are yarrow, rhubarb, and even hops to create a bitter profile.

Curative distilled herbal liqueurs were the domain of the monks, like the Carthusians, best known for concocting chartreuse liqueur and *génépi* aperitif using alpine herbs. The monks started making these alchemical elixirs, thought to prolong the life of the drinker, in the 17th century in the Rhone Alps using more than a hundred different herbs. While not entirely bitter, they laid the foundation for future aperitifs and digestifs.

While there are no clinically proven medicinal benefits of bitter liqueurs, there certainly remains a social one: watching your friends' faces when they have their first sip.

160

DON'T FERNET THE PAST

history

During Prohibition in the United States, fernet was allowed to be sold as a medicine. It's said that upon tasting it, agents from the Alcohol, Tobacco, and Firearms Bureau found it so repulsive that they couldn't imagine anyone drinking it for pleasure, and therefore they allowed it to be sold. The bitter, spiced, and minty liqueur is certainly an acquired taste, but one we dare you not to like after trying it a few times.

161

GET TO KNOW THE CREATORS

⤞➔ One of the earliest renditions of the modern bitter was developed in the mid-19th century by Gaëtan Picon when he was serving in the French Army. With his feverish comrades suffering from waterborne and malarial infections in Algeria, Picon began experimenting with orange peel, gentian, and cinchona to fight the maladies. He was successful enough to begin commercial production upon his return home, releasing Amer Picon, one of the first French bitter aperitifs.

Meanwhile, in Milan, Gaspare Campari was working on his own aperitivo, a vibrant red concoction of cinchona, herbs, and citrus fruit that promptly took Italy by storm. The popularity of the distinctively hued Campari quickly spread to other countries, and the Americano and Negroni cocktails further promoted the bitter.

Also in Milan, Fernet Branca was devised by Bernardino Branca. Based on a recipe he obtained from a Swedish doctor, his bitter digestivo remains a blend of some 40 ingredients, including saffron, coffee, rhubarb, mint, aloe, and juniper.

These bitters all gave way to regional variations and eventually to today's modern interpretations (based on flavors rather than medicinal qualities). Much like some modern styles of gin, which mellow out the intensity of the juniper, bitter liqueurs are finding creative ways to balance the bitterness or build around the flavor with fruit and unique regional ingredients.

162 | FORMULATE YOUR REMEDY

>>→ While it varies by formula and brand, most bitters are made with some combination of cold or hot infusions, distillation, and combining extracts of botanicals. The alcohol content will vary greatly from brand to brand, as will the color, but the presence of sugar or some kind of sweetener is guaranteed. After all, a spoonful of sugar makes the medicine go down!

163

DRINK TO THE BITTER END

Bitter liqueurs are divided into two basic categories: before or after a meal. The botanical recipes are purported to have effects on the digestive system, either to settle or create an appetite.

APERITIVO/APERITIF
Typically light or bright in color, aperitif liqueurs are usually mixed with soda water, wine, or both as a spritz (see item 068). They're enjoyed before dinner with a snack, pairing remarkably well with nibbles like olives, nuts, and even potato chips.

DIGESTIVO/DIGESTIF
Dark and often more powerfully flavored and sweetened, digestif liqueurs are traditionally drunk neat after a meal, to aid digestion by stimulating the stomach to begin its work.

COCKTAIL BITTERS
While not usually consumed on their own, cocktail bitters are the concentrated, usually unsweetened or minimally sugared versions of bitter liqueurs, and they have plenty in common with their digestif cousins. Many cocktail bitters companies have started making bitter liqueurs based on the same recipes.

164 | CHOOSE YOUR PATIO & POOLSIDE DRINK

Enjoy the warm weather by adding sunshine to your cocktail party.

I'M HOSTING A DAYTIME GARDEN PARTY

I'M HOSTING A NIGHTTIME POOL DANCE PARTY

What time of the day?

Can your friends swim?

They're weak swimmers & the pool is closed

Yup and we'll have a lifeguard

AFTERNOON

BRUNCH

ALL DAY

GIN & TONIC
(SEE 171)

PALOMA
(SEE 171)

PARKER HOUSE
(SEE 174)

BRANDY LIFT
(SEE 181)

PIMM'S CUP
(SEE 171)

CUBA LIBRE
(SEE 171)

LONG ISLAND ICED TEA
(SEE 179)

MOJITO
(SEE 165)

MINT JULEP
(SEE 176)

DST
(SEE 180)

BLOODY MARY
(SEE 183)

SANGRIA
(SEE 177)

WHISKEY & COLA
(SEE 171)

SEX ON THE BEACH
(SEE 186)

MOSCOW MULE (VODKA BUCK)
(SEE 169)

MICHELADA
(SEE 182)

BLACK FRIAR TEA (SEE 175)

WHISKEY HIGHBALL
(SEE 171)

Ok, ok! Geez.

And don't forget to wait an hour after eating before jumping in the pool!

LONELY ISLAND
(SEE 179)

165

MOJITO

While the exact origins of this cocktail are murky, we know it's of Cuban origin. Some legends say that Francis Drake developed a rudimentary version of the cocktail in the 16th century, while others claim that slaves working the Cuban sugarcane fields in the 19th century invented the drink. One thing everyone can agree on is that on a hot day there's nothing better.

15 mint leaves

¾ oz lime

¾ oz simple syrup (1:1)

2 oz light rum

1 oz club soda

Mint sprig and lime wheel to garnish

•➜ *In a mixing glass, muddle mint, lime, and simple syrup with enough force to extract the mint oils but not so much that you rip the leaves.*

•➜ *Fill the glass with ice, and then add rum and soda. Stir to incorporate the flavors, and transfer into a Collins glass. Garnish with mint and lime.*

166 GET MUDDLE-HEADED

⤞ Muddling ingredients may look like nothing more than pulverizing the life out of them, but doing it right is more about adding the freshness of produce to a drink without making your cocktail bitter. Here are some muddling basics from David Nepove:

CHOOSE WISELY Painted or dyed muddlers are a thing of the past. Narrow muddlers mean you will be chasing the ingredients around in the bottom of your glass. I suggest a wide-base muddler.

BE SAFE When muddling ingredients, always use a mixing tin or tempered mixing glass. Not all glassware is designed to take the impact of a muddler, causing small chips of glass to break off, which can be fatal if swallowed. When in doubt, muddle in a tin.

CARRY A BIG STICK

167

Muddling requires some force, but it's not a marathon sport. With enough pressure from your muddler you can muddle mint and berries in 3–5 passes, and for ingredients like cucumber, jalapeño, and citrus, 5–10 forceful twists should suffice. Beware of over- or under-doing it: Muddling too much can create a bitter cocktail (or simply be a waste of time), and muddling not enough can leave your drink bland.

•➔ **STEP ONE** Place all ingredients in a mixing tin or tempered glass with your sweetener or juice.

•➔ **STEP TWO** Take your muddler in hand and, with force, press down and apply a twisting motion.

•➔ **STEP THREE** If you are muddling a combination of herbs and fruits or vegetables, stagger the process to muddle in stages. Start with the firmest of the ingredients, giving it a couple of muddles, then adding the second-firmest ingredient, and so on, until you finish off with the most delicate items, such as herbs.

168 BUCK LIKE A MULE

 There's a whole category of cocktails that use ginger beer or ginger ale, but the two most common terms that pop up on cocktail menus are bucks and mules. Both describe a similar combination of ginger beer or ginger ale, liquor, and citrus juice—although technically, the term "buck" has been around much longer (mules are a more recent marketing invention). The Moscow Mule is the best known of the category, but any spirit works in place of the vodka—rum is a particularly good swap.

169

THE MOSCOW MULE (OR VODKA BUCK)

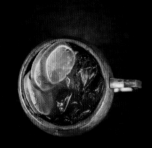

Created as a way to sell vodka in the 1940s, the Moscow Mule has become popular once again. The zesty combination of ginger beer, lime, and vodka served in a glistening copper mug, frosting over as you drink it, hits every Pavlovian trigger on a hot day.

2 oz vodka (or other spirit)

7 oz ginger beer or 1½ oz of homemade ginger syrup (see item 170) with 6 oz of seltzer water

2 lime wedges

•→ *In a Collins glass or copper mug with ice, add the vodka and ginger mixture, then squeeze and drop in the two lime wedges. Give it a stir and serve.*

170   CURE WHAT ALES YOU

You might be tempted to use ginger ale if you can't find ginger beer, but please refrain. Ginger beer has the necessary ginger intensity for bucks and mules, which will otherwise taste watered down. Ginger ale will only add to the watered-down taste—and ginger beer isn't hard to find, as most varieties are nonalcoholic. Luckily, in the absence of ginger beer, making your own ginger brew is easy and also allows you to tailor the strength to your taste (some of us agree that the more ginger, the better). All you need is 1 cup sugar, ½ cup water, a 3 oz ginger root (about the size of a large finger), and 2 pinches salt.

•→ **STEP ONE** Carefully wash the ginger, making sure to rinse away any dirt. Grate the unpeeled ginger on the small perforations (if using a box grater) into a bowl.

•→ **STEP TWO** Place the shredded ginger into a fine strainer, then drain the ginger juice into a jam or mason jar, pressing the solids with your hands or a small spatula to extract as much liquid as possible. Set the juice aside in the fridge, and reserve the ginger solids.

•→ **STEP THREE** In a small pot, combine the sugar and water over medium heat until the combination comes to a boil. Lower the temperature to simmer, stirring in the ginger solids and salt. Allow to simmer together 5 minutes. Remove from heat, cover with a lid, and allow to cool.

•→ **STEP FOUR** Once the sugar syrup is cool, strain into the mason jar with the ginger juice, pressing the solids through a fine strainer again. Cover and shake the jar to combine the juice and syrup together. To mix your own ginger soda, simply combine 1 part ginger syrup to 4 parts seltzer water.

{ MIX UP THE FORMULA }

Here are a few of the many, many ways you can mix spirit and soda and come out on top.

COCKTAIL	LIQUOR	SODA	NOTES
Cuba Libre	Light or dark rum	Cola	Squeeze a lime wedge and drop it into the drink.
Whiskey & Cola	Whiskey	Cola	Keep it simple with no garnishes, although this drink often calls for a higher ratio of cola.
Pimm's Cup	Pimm's Cup	Lemon-lime soda or ginger beer	Garnish with cucumber, mint, fruit, or anything that feels appropriate for a hot-weather garden party.
Paloma	Tequila	Grapefruit soda	Add a pinch of salt and squeeze a lime wedge into the drink.
Gin & Tonic	Gin	Tonic	Pretty easy. Add a squeezed lime wedge.
Vodka & Soda	Vodka	Club soda	See above, and don't be fooled into thinking it's a low-calorie option (a standard glass of wine has fewer). Try a mocktail (see item 231) if you want to keep things light.
Whiskey Highball	Blended Japanese whisky	Club soda	This will work with other whiskies, but Japanese whisky is designed to work well with a little water (a process called *mizuwari*).

172

BE THE YODA OF SODA

One of the easiest ways to mix a drink is to combine some type of bubbly soda with your favorite spirit. The basic ratio of one part liquor to two parts soda is a good place to start—but don't feel like you can't adjust the recipe. On hot days, often the best balance can be closer to three parts soda for one of liquor, making it more refreshing without overdiluting the spirit. Gin & tonics, in particular, often benefit from going a little heavier on the tonic water, depending on the brand.

2 oz spirit of your choice
4 oz soda of your choice

•→ *In a Collins or highball glass with ice, add the liquor and then the soda. Add a straw and give it a quick stir, garnishing if called for.*

✦ MATT COWAN ✦

Cocktail Curator | La Cour Denver's Art Bar

173

CHERRY BLOSSOM

This take on a Japanese highball gets a vibrant jolt of acidity from the vinegar and lemon, and a cherry blossom pink hue and flavor from cherry liqueur. It's the perfect toast to spring's new blossoms.

1½ oz Japanese whisky
(Hibiki or Iwai blended preferred)

¾ oz lemon juice

1 oz simple syrup (1:1)

½ oz cherry liqueur

¼ oz raspberry vinegar

Soda water

Pink-red edible flower or cherries speared on a cocktail pick to garnish

•◂ *Combine the whisky, lemon juice, simple syrup, cherry liqueur, and vinegar in a cocktail shaker with ice. Shake hard 8–10 seconds and strain into a Collins or highball glass with fresh ice. Top with the soda water and stir in gently. Garnish with flower or cherries.*

H. JOSEPH EHRMANN ✦ Owner/Operator | Elixir Saloon

174 { PARKER HOUSE COCKTAIL }

This variation of a French 75 and a Boothby cocktail evolved into a tall, refreshing drink with a large dose of sparkling wine. Typically, a drink like this would be stirred for a silky texture, but here it's shaken—for the sake of speed, and because the sparkling wine adds more texture than the spirits.

1 oz rye whiskey
(Rittenhouse 100 preferred)

1 oz Cognac

1 oz sweet vermouth
(Antica Formula preferred)

2 dashes pimento bitters
(Dale Degroff's preferred)

Demi-sec gewürztraminer sparkling wine

•◂ *Combine rye, cognac, vermouth, and bitters in a cocktail shaker with ice. Shake hard 8–10 seconds and strain into a Collins or highball glass with fresh ice. Top with the sparkling wine and stir in gently.*

USBG | INDIANAPOLIS CHAPTER

✦ JASON FOUST ✦

USBG Midwestern Regional VP

176

MINT JULEP

This variation of the classic Mint Julep is crisp and refreshing, with the whiskey bite softened by a touch of lime juice. The aroma of the mint sets the tone as you drink it, so make sure your sprig is fresh. And remember to hold the drink correctly: the julep cup was designed to be held at the bottom, by the base, so that the sides stay frosty.

4-6 mint leaves

1 oz demerara simple syrup (1:1)

2 oz bourbon whiskey

¼ oz lime juice

Mint sprig to garnish

•❧ *Add enough crushed ice to the julep cup (or old-fashioned glass) to form a mound on top, and set aside to chill. In a cocktail shaker, add the mint and demerara syrup, and very gently press the mint with a muddler to release the aromatic oils. Add bourbon, lime juice, and ice, then gently shake to combine ingredients. Strain into the ice-filled cup and garnish with a mint sprig.*

USBG | TAMPA CHAPTER

JULIAN MILLER ✦ Bartender in Residence | Partender

175 ⟩ BLACK FRIAR TEA

When you want a Pimm's Cup with an extra kick of gin, try this variation. The name is an homage to the Black Friar monks who have been distilling Plymouth gin for more than two centuries. Despite the good measure of gin, the cocktail is extremely versatile and refreshing.

2 oz Plymouth gin

1⅓ oz Pimm's No. 1

⅔ oz aperitivo liqueur

3 oz ginger beer (see item 170 to make your own)

Lemon and lime wheel to garnish

•❧ *In a Collins or highball glass with ice, add the gin, Pimm's, aperitivo liqueur, and then the ginger beer. Add a straw and give it a quick stir, garnishing with the citrus wheels.*

•❧ *If you don't have a ⅓ ounce measure on your jiggers, remember that ⅓ ounce is equal to 2 teaspoons!*

177 { SINGLE-SERVING SANGRIA }

Occasionally, you won't want to make a big batch of sangria just to get a glass or two to enjoy in the garden on an unexpectedly chore-free afternoon. The key to this drink is the fruit garnish, so use whatever you have handy: sliced citrus, strawberries, peaches, apples, or anything ripe and in season. Without the fruit, it's just a wine cocktail.

3 oz cheap and cheerful red wine

1½ oz orange liqueur (or ½ oz rich simple syrup for a less boozy option)

½ oz fruit liqueur (berry liqueurs works great)

½ oz lemon juice

1 oz juice (orange or your favorite)

1 oz soda water

Sliced fruit to garnish

•❥ Combine the red wine, orange liqueur, fruit liqueur, lemon, and juice in a cocktail shaker with ice. Shake hard 8–10 seconds and strain into a Collins or highball glass with fresh ice. Top with the soda water and stir in gently. Garnish with fruit.

178

WHIP UP A WHITE SANGRIA

White sangria is an easy and delicious alternative, although you'll need to make a few minor tweaks to the recipe. Use 4 ounces white wine instead of the red wine, and try using peach or apricot liqueur instead of berry.

USBG | INDIANAPOLIS CHAPTER

✦ JASON FOUST ✦

USBG Midwestern Regional VP

179

LONELY ISLAND

Designed as a way to make mezcal approachable to newcomers, this drink uses ingredients that tame the smoky profile of mezcal. Coconut is a great pairing for smoky flavors, and the jalapeño adds a vegetal element with a kick.

1½ oz mezcal (Del Maguey VIDA preferred)

½ oz jalapeño-infused simple syrup (1:1)

½ oz Coco Reàl syrup

½ oz lime juice

2 dashes Bittercube Jamaican #1 bitters

Jalapeño slice to garnish

•❥ Combine all ingredients except garnish in a cocktail shaker with ice. Shake 8–10 seconds and strain into a Collins or highball glass with fresh ice. Garnish with the jalapeño slice.

180

DST

A shandy is a style of drink in which beer is mixed with soda or other sweeteners; the DST leans more toward a cocktail, with tangy and citrus-forward flavors and fruity undertones. The gin and IPA give the drink some edge, while the maraschino and orange marmalade bring depth and balance. The rest of the ingredients help to bind and pull out certain flavors. The name refers to the extra hour of sunlight that daylight saving time brings into the day.

1½ oz gin (Fords preferred)

¾ oz maraschino liqueur

½ oz lemon juice

2 teaspoons sweet orange marmalade

2 dashes orange bitters

Your favorite citrus-forward IPA beer

Lemon slice

•➔ *Combine gin, maraschino liqueur, lemon, marmalade, and bitters in a cocktail shaker with ice. Shake hard 8–10 seconds (to incorporate the marmalade) and double-strain into a pint glass with fresh ice. Top with the beer and stir in gently. Garnish with a lemon slice.*

✦ JENNIFER COLLIAU ✦

Owner of Small Hand Foods

181

BRANDY LIFT

The Brandy Lift cocktail is based around a love for New York–style egg creams and a challenge to combine Cognac and Benedictine with one of the cocktail syrups that Jennifer Colliau produces at Small Hand Foods. The recipe is unusual because cream and seltzer cocktails usually contain eggs; since this is not quite a flip, she came up with the old-timey (but very modern) name "lift."

1½ oz Cognac or good brandy

½ oz Small Hand Foods orgeat

½ oz Benedictine liqueur

½ oz heavy cream

Seltzer to top

•➔ *Combine the brandy, orgeat, Benedictine, and heavy cream in a cocktail shaker with ice. Shake hard 8–10 seconds and strain into a chilled Collins or highball glass with fresh ice. Use a barspoon to paddle the drink furiously back and forth while adding seltzer to the rim of the glass. Let sit a minute or two to firm up the head, then slowly drizzle in more seltzer to lift the head above the rim of the drink. Serve with a straw.*

183

BLOODY MARY

For many, the Bloody Mary is the pizza of cocktails—in that some are more concerned with the garnishes and toppings than the actual beverage. Here's how to make a good one—and decorate as you desire.

2 oz vodka or blanco tequila

4 oz tomato juice

1 oz lemon juice

½ teaspoon horseradish, grated

2-3 dashes Worcestershire sauce

Tabasco to taste

2 dashes celery salt

2 dashes black pepper

An assortment of pickled veggies to garnish

•❥ *Combine all ingredients except garnish in a cocktail shaker and roll the drink from one tin to another in order to combine. Strain into a pint glass filled with ice, and garnish with the veggies of your choice.*

•❥ *Note: If you have a little advance notice for a brunch gathering, you can make a big batch of Bloody Marys for the following day. Simply combine everything except the liquor and let it sit overnight. Like soup, the flavors will marry, delivering an improved and harmonized drink.*

182 ◈ MICHELADA

The Michelada may sound like nothing more than the beer version of a Bloody Mary, but this cocktail varies widely—from a simple combination of lime, salt, and beer to more complicated brunch affairs. While we're not shy about having a cocktail in the morning, sometimes you need something lighter to limber yourself up.

Salt or Tajín to rim the glass

3 oz tomato juice (or Clamato)

2 oz lime juice

4 dashes Maggi seasoning sauce (or soy sauce)

3 dashes hot sauce (bottled Mexican, Tabasco, or Crystal—or even sriracha—work here), or more if you like the heat

1 fat pinch salt

12 oz can Mexican beer or lager, ice cold

•❥ *Place enough salt (or Tajín, the Mexican chile-and-citrus salt blend) to create a thin layer on a small plate. Moisten the lip of a pint glass with a lime wedge, then dip and twirl the glass to coat the rim. Set the glass aside.*

•❥ *Add ice to the glass, then the tomato juice, lime juice, Maggi, hot sauce, and salt. Stir, then add as much beer as will fit, leaving a few fingers of space at the top.*

184

LONG ISLAND ICED TEA

Enjoying a cocktail should be like a nice stroll on the beach—a chance to slow down, take your time, and enjoy yourself. Some cocktails, however, are by design less of a leisurely walk and more like base-jumping off an active volcano—built for speed and often ending poorly for the participant. The merits of the Long Island Iced Tea are that it doesn't taste bad at all (contrary to all logic), and that it's a good drink to know how to mix—since someone, at some point, will ask you to make one.

½ oz vodka

½ oz tequila

½ oz white rum

½ oz gin

½ oz triple sec

½ oz lemon juice

½ oz simple syrup (1:1)

Splash of cola to top off

Lemon wedge or twist to garnish

•→ *Add all ingredients except cola and lemon garnish to a Collins glass with ice. Top off with a splash of cola and garnish with the lemon.*

185 { ENDLESSLY VARY THE FORMULA }

The Long Island Iced Tea comes in many, many variations; most of them are simple tweaks on the original. The endless varieties allow bars and hosts to create their own branded spin—easy and adaptable. Just make sure your guests don't overimbibe. As any college student will tell you, this tea can get you into trouble. Here's a small sampling to get your juices (and liquors) flowing.

LONG BEACH
Uses cranberry juice instead of cola

TEXAS ICED TEA
Adds ½ oz Bourbon to the recipe

ADIOS MOTHER F*CKER
Blue curaçao replaces the triple sec, and uses lemon-lime soda stands in for the cola

GEORGIA ICED TEA
Uses peach liqueur in place of the triple sec

HAWAIIAN ICED TEA
Replaces cola with pineapple juice

THREE MILE ISLAND
Midori melon liqueur replaces the cola (adding a distinctive nuclear green color)

---

186 | HAVE SEX ON THE BEACH

The Sex on the Beach may be a member of the infamous oeuvre of drinks that are ordered for the sake of their name rather than the quality of the spirit, but it doesn't make for a bad drink, especially in the right situation (and no, a first date is not the right situation).

1½ oz vodka

½ oz peach liqueur

1½ oz orange juice

1½ oz cranberry juice

Orange wedge or twist to garnish

•➤ *Add all ingredients except the garnish to a Collins glass with ice. Garnish with the orange.*

---

187 | KNOW YOUR FETISHES

There are just as many twists on the classic Sex on the Beach. Here are three notables:

SEX ON FIRE Uses cinnamon-infused whiskey (like Fireball) in place of the vodka

MADRAS Uses only vodka (2 oz total) without the liqueur

WOO WOO This variation gets straight to the point and ditches the orange juice altogether

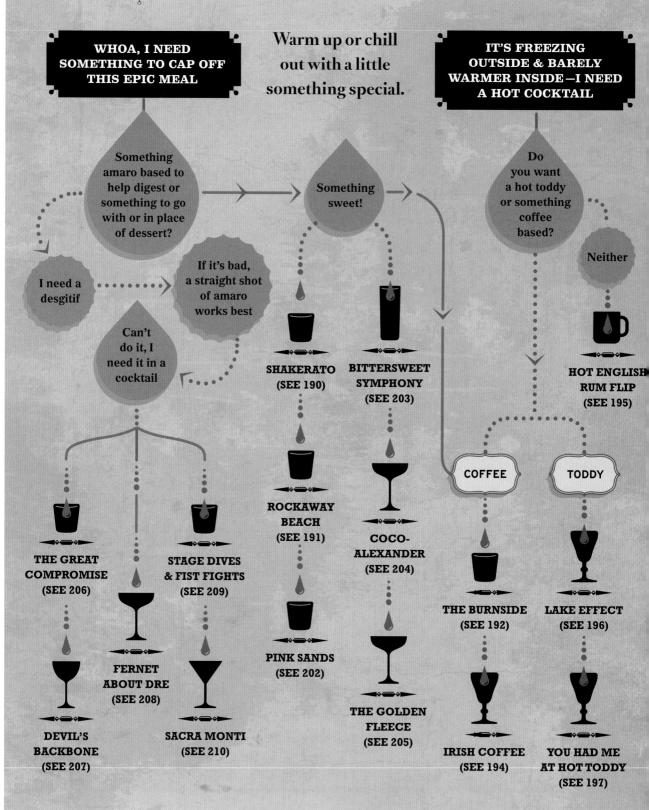

WHOA, I NEED SOMETHING TO CAP OFF THIS EPIC MEAL

Warm up or chill out with a little something special.

IT'S FREEZING OUTSIDE & BARELY WARMER INSIDE—I NEED A HOT COCKTAIL

Something amaro based to help digest or something to go with or in place of dessert?

Something sweet!

Do you want a hot toddy or something coffee based?

Neither

I need a desgitif

If it's bad, a straight shot of amaro works best

Can't do it, I need it in a cocktail

SHAKERATO (SEE 190)

BITTERSWEET SYMPHONY (SEE 203)

HOT ENGLISH RUM FLIP (SEE 195)

COFFEE

TODDY

THE GREAT COMPROMISE (SEE 206)

STAGE DIVES & FIST FIGHTS (SEE 209)

ROCKAWAY BEACH (SEE 191)

COCO-ALEXANDER (SEE 204)

THE BURNSIDE (SEE 192)

LAKE EFFECT (SEE 196)

FERNET ABOUT DRE (SEE 208)

PINK SANDS (SEE 202)

DEVIL'S BACKBONE (SEE 207)

SACRA MONTI (SEE 210)

THE GOLDEN FLEECE (SEE 205)

IRISH COFFEE (SEE 194)

YOU HAD ME AT HOT TODDY (SEE 197)

189  PULL SHOTS LIKE A BARISTA

Lured by the gleaming espresso machine at Americano, bartender Kate Bolton incorporated coffee into her cocktails by turning traditional espresso drinks into something perfect for postwork. Dust off that espresso machine and shake yourself awake.

190

SHAKERATO

The Shakerato is a classic Italian drink to be enjoyed on hot days, usually made by shaking espresso and simple syrup with ice. This version gets wired with Italian amaro and creamy dairy additions.

1 oz espresso

1 oz Melletti amaro

½ oz half and half

Combine all ingredients in a cocktail shaker. Add ice, shake hard 8–10 seconds, and strain into a small rocks or old-fashioned glass.

191 { ROCKAWAY BEACH }

Since one of the founders of Americano, Blair Reynolds, also owns the tiki bar Hale Pele, Bolton wanted to bridge the coffee and tiki culture in one cocktail. This simple combination allows coconut to stand out while the strong, funky backbone of Jamaican pot-still rum plays with the earthy qualities of the coffee.

2 oz cold-brew coffee

1 oz coconut milk

¾ oz Smith and Cross Jamaican Rum

¾ oz rich demerara syrup (2:1)

Half orange wheel sprinkled with shredded coconut

Combine the coffee, coconut milk, rum, and demerara syrup in a cocktail shaker. Add ice, shake hard 8–10 seconds, and strain into a rocks or old-fashioned glass with ice. Garnish with the half orange wheel sprinkled with shredded coconut.

192 THE BURNSIDE

This drink was created by Americano bartender Eric Rickey as a play on the classic combination of mint and chocolate in a hot coffee drink. The Fernet Branca Menta is a very minty version of the Italian amaro, and the Mud Puddle Bitter Chocolate vodka is made by local Portland distillery New Deal.

1½ oz Fernet Branca Menta

½ oz Mud Puddle Bitter Chocolate vodka

1½ oz espresso

3 oz steamed milk

Cocoa to garnish

Mint leaf

Add Fernet, vodka, and espresso to an Irish coffee or double-walled coffee glass, then add hot steamed milk. Garnish with a sprinkling of cocoa and mint leaf.

193 ⊹ UNDERSTAND IRISH WHISKEY

First introduced by Christian monks, the Irish smartly distinguished their whiskey from Scotch by developing a cleaner, floral, and fruity whiskey that comes in a variety of styles. *Single-pot still whiskey* is a unique style in which a mix of both malted and unmalted grains are distilled in a pot still. Pot-distilled *single malt* is made from malted barley and also *blended whiskey* that combines single malt or single-pot still whiskies with grain whiskey (made from unmalted grain in a continuous still). A large majority of the popular Irish whiskies are blended.

194

IRISH COFFEE

An easy-drinking hot cup of coffee sweetened with a little sugar and braced with a shot of Irish whiskey, the Irish Coffee is an ageless classic. Originally created by a County Limerick chef for weather-weary travelers in the 1940s, the drink has spread around the world.

1½ oz Irish whiskey	For the cream:
3 oz coffee	2 oz heavy cream
2 teaspoons sugar	1½ teaspoons sugar

In a chilled shaker, combine the heavy cream and 1½ teaspoons sugar, and shake until the cream thickens and the sugar dissolves. You don't need stiff peaks—nor butter (which will happen if you shake too long). Set aside.

Combine remaining ingredients in an Irish Coffee glass and stir to combine. Top with a float of cream.

195 { HOT ENGLISH RUM FLIP }

This old-timey concoction is a little like a hot eggnog but without the dairy. Originally made by plunging a hot piece of metal, called a loggerhead, into an ale mug, this version goes a little more modern by using the stovetop.

2 oz rum

1 large egg

1 tablespoon sweetener of your choice (molasses or sorghum preferred)

6 oz English-style beer (or a dark beer)

Nutmeg, to grate

•➤ *Make a small ring with a kitchen towel and place a small metal bowl into it, making sure it fits snugly. Add the rum, egg, and sweetener into the bowl and whisk until combined.*

•➤ *Add beer to a saucepan and heat until the beer begins to simmer. Remove from heat. While whisking the rum-egg mixture, slowly add the hot beer.*

•➤ *Ladle into a mug and grate nutmeg over drink.*

USBG | INDIANAPOLIS CHAPTER

✦ JASON FOUST ✦

USBG Midwestern Regional VP

196 | LAKE EFFECT

Named after the heavy snow caused by the winds coming off the Great Lakes in the Midwest, this variation on a hot toddy will keep you cozy when you are stuck inside. Or outside.

1½ oz whiskey (Tincup preferred)

½ oz Bitter Truth pimento dram

½ oz ginger syrup

½ oz lemon juice

2 oz hot water

Cracked black pepper

•➤ *Combine all ingredients except pepper into a coffee mug and stir. Garnish with freshly cracked black pepper.*

USBG | ATLANTA CHAPTER

✦ IAN COX ✦

Craft Spirit Specialist | National Distributing

197 | YOU HAD ME AT HOT TODDY

This toddy variation was developed for a 750-person event; on a lark, Ian decided to serve a hot drink. While November in Atlanta can still be beautiful, the weather was miserably cold and rainy. The name stuck when a young woman screamed, "You had me at hot toddy!"

1½ oz bourbon

2½ oz hot vanilla black tea

¼ oz fernet (Vittone Menta preferred)

Orange peel

•➤ *Combine all ingredients except orange peel in an Irish Coffee glass and stir to combine. Express orange peel over the top and place in drink.*

BRANDY

BRANDY LIES IN AN INTERSECTION OF VINICULTURE AND AGRICULTURE, ENCOMPASSING EVERYTHING FROM COGNAC AND GRAPPA TO APPLEJACK AND SLIVOVITZ.

198

KNOW THE HISTORY

➤ In the 9th century, the distillation process was developed with wine, making brandy the first liquor ever distilled. Initially used for medicinal purposes, the popularity of cognac and Armagnac brandy soared in the 15th and 16th centuries, as Dutch traders began to export unaged grape eau-de-vie in barrels.

That trade began to transform brandy. No longer a potent spirit to be watered down or used to fortify wines for shipment, it was now defined as an aged spirit. The traveling added a negligible amount of wood age, and soon fluctuations in demand and production led to more oak making its way in.

But brandy is more than just cognac or Armagnac. The general definition of brandy is a spirit made from distilled fruit. Any fruit could be used to produce a type of brandy, and in large part it developed as an agrarian tool to preserve bumper crops or, in some cases, to utilize fruits that were too bitter or acidic.

The best brandies don't usually share fruit with the best wines. Grape-based brandies like cognac and Armagnac are primarily made of ugni blanc (also known as Trebbiano), folle Blanche, and Colombard grapes, which yield thin, acidic wine. Calvados often incorporates bitter, aromatic apples, and eau-de-vie brandies are best made from fruit varieties that need cooking or processing to make them palatable. Unlike with wine, the skin of the fruit is as important as the flesh when it comes to brandies for flavor and aroma.

199

KNOW YOUR FRENCH FRIED VINES

In the late 19th century, an aphid pest called phylloxera, which feeds off grapevines and destroys the roots in the process, started attacking French vineyards. The pest practically annihilated the wine and brandy industries, destroying nearly half of all vineyards in France. The Great French Wine Blight thus created a shift in the way people made cocktails. With supplies of French brandies devastated, Europe and the United States developed a taste for gin along with whiskies—and began drinking cocktails featuring those spirits.

200 | LEARN THE PROCESS

Brandy production always starts with fruit in some form, with the style defining how its fermented, if and for how long it is aged, and what kinds of distillation are allowed.

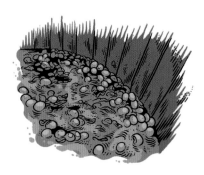

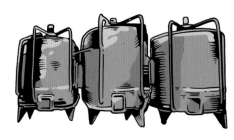

•➔ STEP ONE The fruit is crushed to allow the juices (and, most important, the sugars) in the flesh to be extracted and come in contact with wild or cultivated yeast. Sometimes the juice alone is fermented, while other recipes use the whole mash with water added to facilitate fermentation.

•➔ STEP TWO The fermentation of the fruit can last anywhere from a few days to many weeks, depending on the conditions. Often the fermentation is cooled in order to control the type of yeasts that thrive, a process that also lengthens the fermentation time.

•➔ STEP THREE The fruit mash or wine is distilled. Most aged brandies are pot distilled, but some, like Armagnac, are distilled once through a special column to achieve a moderately low proof of about 52–60 percent. Neutral brandy for fortification is often distilled through columns, leading to a much higher proof.

201

IDENTIFY THE TYPES

Brandy is determined not only by its fruit but by its process and uses. Here are the three types of brandy to know.

WINE BRANDY The most commonly associated subcategory with the term "brandy" are the aged grape-based varieties like cognac, Spanish jerez, and Armagnac; but anywhere wine grapes are grown, you'll find a tradition of the aged spirit—such as in Italy, Greece, Turkey, Armenia, Cyprus, South Africa, and the United States (primarily in California). The wine brandies also include unaged spirits like Pisco from Peru and Chile.

POMACE BRANDY This style is also grape-based, but it's focused on economizing the winemaking process by utilizing the leftover solids (or pomace). Originally the staple of vineyard workers, pomace-based brandies—like the infamous Italian grappa—can be found in most winemaking regions. There are unique and refined brandies to be found here, so don't pass it all off as rotgut.

FRUIT BRANDY A bit of a catchall category, fruit brandy includes aged brandies like Calvados and applejack, as well as unaged eau-de-vie like Poire Williams (pear), kirsch (cherry), and many other varieties of the fruit distillates. When well made, they boast the many aromas and flavors of fresh fruit (without the sugar and acidity) that make them great digestifs—or flavorings for desserts. Be sure to read the label when buying fruit brandies, as some inexpensive brands are actually just artificially flavored grape brandy and not made from the fruit that might be on the label.

✦ MONICA SNYDER ✦

Sales Representative | Glazer's Distributors

202 ◈ PINK SANDS

Hailing from South Padre Island, Texas, Monica Snyder wanted to create a drink that reminded her of the beach and also tasted like a beach drink. Don't forget the suntan lotion.

1 oz coconut rum

½ oz rye whiskey

¼ oz raspberry liqueur

4 oz coconut milk

Dash of simple syrup (1:1)

Cherry and umbrella to garnish

•❧ *Combine all ingredients except garnish in a cocktail shaker. Add ice, shake hard 8–10 seconds, and strain into a large rocks or old-fashioned glass with crushed ice. Garnish with a cherry and umbrella.*

RICH WILLIAMS ✦ Bartender | The Spare Room

203 ◈ BITTERSWEET SYMPHONY

After touring a gin distillery, bartender Rich Williams visited an ice cream shop that offered Negroni ice cream—and so the idea for this drink was formed. The balance of bitter and creamy, sweet flavors make this rich drink a dessert and cocktail in one.

2 oz gin

¾ oz bianco (or blanc) vermouth

½ oz heavy cream

½ oz egg white

½ oz aperitivo liqueur (like Campari)

¾ oz simple syrup (1:1)

Mint leaves and cherry to garnish

•❧ *Combine all ingredients except garnish in a cocktail shaker. Add ice, shake hard 8–10 seconds, and strain into a Collins or highball glass. Top with crushed ice and garnish with mint and cherry.*

✦ MATT COWAN ✦

Cocktail Curator | La Cour

204 ◈

COCO-ALEXANDER

Aside from being vegan, this version of the Brandy Alexander has the added advantage of not curdling with tart liqueurs, such as raspberry. If you prefer the dairy version, simply swap out the coconut for heavy cream.

Toasted coconut

Lemon wedge

1½ oz dry vermouth infused with rhubarb

1 oz crème de cacao or other liqueur

1 oz unsweetened coconut cream (not cream of coconut, which is sweetened)

•❧ *On a small plate, place enough coconut to create a thin layer. Moisten the rim of a coupe or cocktail glass by running a lemon wedge around the lip, then dip and twirl the glass into the coconut to coat half of the glass rim. Set the glass aside.*

•❧ *Combine the remaining ingredients in a shaker. Add ice, shake hard 8–10 seconds, and strain into the prepared glass.*

✦ NAT HARRY ✦

Spirits Buyer for Cask

205

THE GOLDEN FLEECE

Named after the golden coat of the mythical winged ram, this cocktail carries a similar sheen—with a spicy kick, like a quick hoof to the face. Assemble your own Argonauts and set off to find this gilded treasure.

1¾ oz aged cachaça (Avuá Amburana preferred)

¾ oz sweetened condensed milk

¼ oz Ancho Reyes liqueur (spicy dried pepper liqueur)

1 dash chocolate bitters (Fee Brothers Aztec chocolate bitters preferred)

Cinnamon stick, to grate

•➔ *Combine all ingredients except cinnamon in a cocktail shaker. Add ice, shake 8–10 seconds, and strain into a cold coupe or wine glass. Garnish with freshly grated cinnamon.*

✦ **MATTHEW KORZELIUS** ✦

Barman | Manna

206

THE GREAT COMPROMISE

After realizing that cola was originally a style of sweet amaro (with the flavors built from a blend of botanicals), Matthew Korzelius started thinking about pairing it with other Italian digestives. The name refers to the middle line where bitter flavors (often an acquired taste) are mixed into something more approachable.

¾ oz cola reduction

1½ oz bourbon whiskey

½ oz fernet

¾ oz Punt é Mes vermouth

2 dashes cherry bitters

Cherry to garnish

•✦ *To make the cola reduction, simmer store-bought cola over medium heat until reduced to about ⅙ its original volume; let cool.*

•✦ *Combine all ingredients except garnish in a cocktail shaker. Add ice, shake hard 8–10 seconds, and strain into a rocks or old-fashioned glass with a large ice cube. Garnish with a cherry on top.*

CHRIS LANE ✦ Bar Manager | Ramen Shop

207 { DEVIL'S BACKBONE }

This cocktail is a bracer, best enjoyed after a big meal, a long day of work, or by anyone who loves big, smoky flavors and a little bitter with the sweet. Based on the smoky whiskies his dad drank (for which Chris gained an early appreciation), this cocktail is a blend of two whiskies, two amari, and two bitters. Rich and heavy with just enough bitterness balanced with sweetness, it ends a meal like a nap by the fireplace.

1 oz rye whiskey

½ oz Ardbeg 10-year single malt (or other smoky Scotch)

¾ oz Averna amaro

½ oz Gran Classico (or other aperitivo liqueur)

1 dash aromatic bitters (Angostura preferred)

1 dash orange bitters (Bitter Truth preferred)

Orange peel disc to garnish

•✦ *Combine all ingredients except garnish in a pint or mixing glass, add ice, and stir 20–30 seconds. Strain the cocktail into a Nick and Nora or small coupe or cocktail glass. Express orange peel over drink and garnish with the peel side up on the surface.*

✦ RYAN SHIPMAN ✦

Bar Manager

208

FERNET ABOUT DRE

While minty fernet is often taken as a digestive, here it's combined with another Italian-style amaro, floral with saffron, anise, and violets. The black walnut bitters bridges the gap between the whiskey and the amari to make for a strong post-feast tipple.

2 oz rye whiskey

¾ oz fernet

¾ oz Meletti amaro

2 dashes Fee Brothers black walnut bitters

Cherry to garnish

Add all ingredients except garnish into a glass pitcher, add ice, and stir 30 seconds. Double-strain into a coupe glass. Garnish with a cherry.

✦ STEPHAN MENDEZ ✦

Beverage Director

The Boulevardier Group

209

STAGE DIVES & FIST FIGHTS

Named after the imagined bad behavior too many of these boozy, tequila-based cocktails might inspire, this drink is not for the weak. The crown garnish is designed to be a fun touch, and is appropriate considering this drink's popularity has kept it on The Last Word bar's cocktail menu a record three time in a row. It really is the king of the ring.

1½ oz blanco tequila

¾ oz Pedro Ximénez sherry

¾ oz sweet vermouth

2 dashes cardamom bitters

Orange peel, cut into the shape of a crown

•➔ *Combine all ingredients except orange peel in a rocks or old-fashioned glass, add ice, and stir. Garnish with an orange peel crown.*

ALEJANDRO OLIVARES ✦ Bartender | Under Current

210 { SACRA MONTI }

This cocktail is named after the series of sculptures and religious shrines that runs along the Italian mountain range connecting Lombardo and Piedmont, where Zucca amaro and Cocchi vermouth di Torino originate. It's a little bitter, a little herbal, and it comes with a cherry dessert.

1½ oz bourbon
(Buffalo Trace preferred)

½ oz sweet vermouth
(Cocchi preferred)

½ oz Zucca amaro
(rhubarb bitter liqueur)

3 dashes aromatic bitters
(like Angostura)

Cherry to garnish

•➔ *Combine all ingredients except garnish in a cocktail shaker. Add ice, shake hard 8–10 seconds, and strain into a coupe or cocktail glass. Pinch the lemon peel over the drink (to express the citrus oils) and then drop it in the glass.*

Entertaining & Hospitality

Y ou probably have a favorite bar or local watering hole, and chances are good that part of the reason you like the place has something to do with how comfortable and welcomed you feel—not just the quality of the drinks.

Sure, recipes are important, but even if your host knows how to mix every classic recipe, it won't necessarily make for a bar or party you'll enjoy being at. Hospitality, proper planning, and keeping guests happy and upright (so they remember how much fun they had) are as important to a great bar as the recipes.

Here we apply some pro hospitality techniques to hosting your next event. Learn how to build a perfect drink menu, make your drinks look photo-ready, and even mix great mocktails. Being a good host will make your parties that much more fun for your guests and easier for you to enjoy.

Not sure where to start? Check out item 213 to get started.

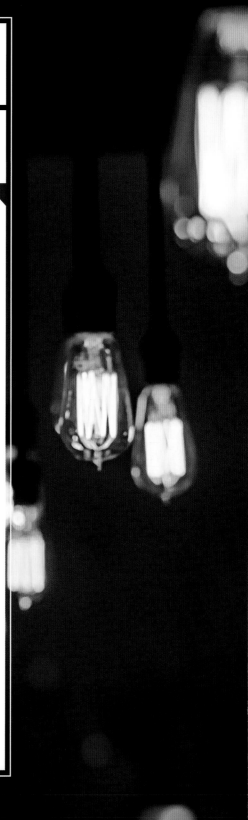

211 ❧ BE THE HOST WITH THE MOST

 When it comes to hospitality, we're not saying that you need to act like you're running a bar when you have your friends over for drinks (unless they tip well). But there are some things to glean from the way bartenders think about service, so Ted Kilgore of Planter's House gave us some tips on the kinds of things he and his staff think about when serving guests.

•➤ KNOW YOUR AUDIENCE It may seem obvious, but busting out the high-end craft cocktails made with bitter Italian amaros when you're having your grandma over with other family members is probably not the best idea. If they're not happy, you probably won't be, either.

•➤ EARN THEIR TRUST Few people are born cocktail geeks, and most evolve their tastes as they experience new things. Earn their trust—first by giving them what they want instead of what you think they should have, and then graduating to the new and undiscovered. The key is to help people understand the magic of cocktails via things they feel comfortable with.

•➤ BUILD AN ACCESSIBLE MENU Is your new party cocktail a twist on a Manhattan? Make it obvious in the name so that people who like the classic will be drawn to the update. Fanciful names are also fun—just be prepared to explain the drink by comparing it to something else they may know.

•➤ RESEARCH YOUR SPIRITS If you're mixing with an unusual ingredient (always good), try to learn a little bit about it: how it's made, where's it's from, its history, and other interesting tidbits. Even better, be prepared with tasters for your guests.

•➤ PUT ON A SHOW Do your best to make sure guests have a great time. That's why they're here, so embrace the theatrics of the cocktail making, the alchemy of the creation of the drink, and the conversation surrounding it. And don't forget to be a guest at your own party—make sure you've got a drink, too.

212

DEAL WITH DRUNKEN GUESTS

Even the most well-prepared of drinkers will sometimes get a little pickled without meaning to. It happens, and, as a host, it's your responsibility to make sure everyone has a good time and stays safe. Here's what to keep in mind when a friend abruptly goes from tipsy to trashed.

TAKE CARE If a friend is clearly tipsy but not lampshade drunk, make sure he's not driving, arrange a safe ride home, and give him a bottle of water and some solid, heavy snacks to help get him upright again.

MAKE UP THE SOFA If he's really not like himself, seems confused, or is acting irrationally, don't let him leave. The last thing you want is for your buddy to get behind the wheel, pass out in a cab or subway, or get arrested for public intoxication—or worse.

FORGIVE POOR CONDUCT Remember that movie *The Exorcist*? Remember all the mean and manipulative things that the possessed people said? There's a chance a drunken guest may behave in ways that shock you—and he may not have any memory of the episode the next day. Best to forgive and forget, and know that he would be horrified if he knew what a jerk he was. Treat him like you would like to be treated when it happens to you someday.

PREPARE FOR A MESS Remember that other traumatic part of *The Exorcist*? Get a bucket nearby even if your pal doesn't look ready to spew. Remind him repeatedly where it is. Some demons just need to be cast out.

BE PATIENT Forget coffee and all the tricks you've heard for sobering up—the only one that really works is time. Waiting it out can be agonizing, but hopefully everyone will do that while sleeping.

SEE A DOCTOR Beware of alcohol poisoning—if anyone has trouble catching his or her breath or starts breathing irregularly, experiences a change in skin color, or shows any sign of seizures, get him or her to a hospital immediately.

213 | GET READY TO PARTY

Trying to plan your next party? Let us help you come up with some ideas and devise a cocktail strategy. What kind of party were you thinking of hosting?

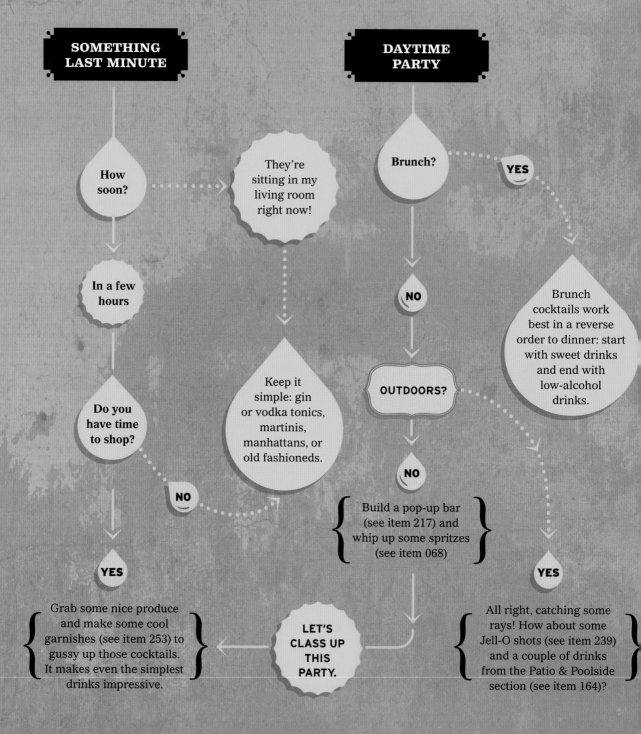

SOMETHING LAST MINUTE

How soon?

They're sitting in my living room right now!

In a few hours

Do you have time to shop?

Keep it simple: gin or vodka tonics, martinis, manhattans, or old fashioneds.

NO

YES

Grab some nice produce and make some cool garnishes (see item 253) to gussy up those cocktails. It makes even the simplest drinks impressive.

LET'S CLASS UP THIS PARTY.

DAYTIME PARTY

Brunch?

YES

NO

OUTDOORS?

NO

Brunch cocktails work best in a reverse order to dinner: start with sweet drinks and end with low-alcohol drinks.

Build a pop-up bar (see item 217) and whip up some spritzes (see item 068)

YES

All right, catching some rays! How about some Jell-O shots (see item 239) and a couple of drinks from the Patio & Poolside section (see item 164)?

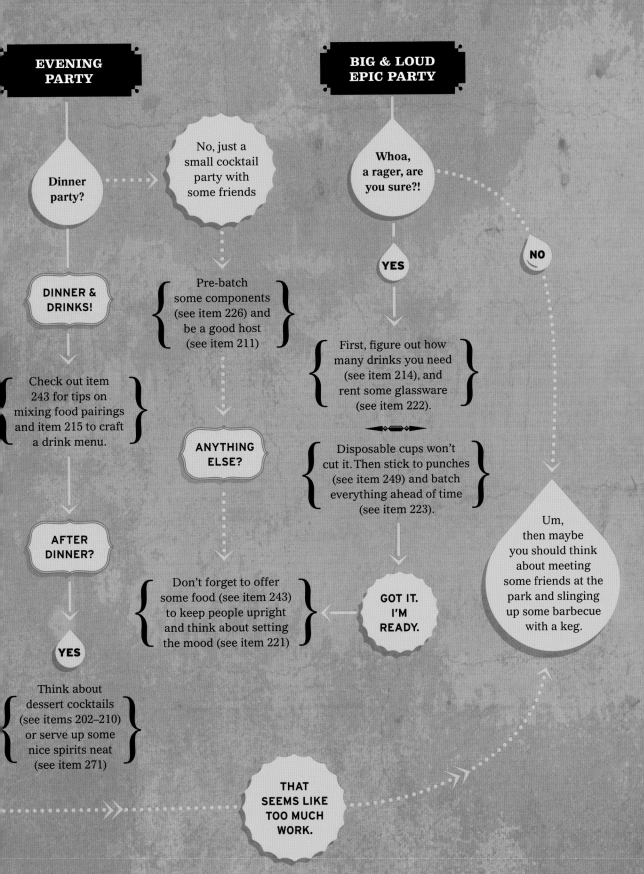

EVENING PARTY

BIG & LOUD EPIC PARTY

Dinner party?

No, just a small cocktail party with some friends

Whoa, a rager, are you sure?!

YES

NO

DINNER & DRINKS!

Pre-batch some components (see item 226) and be a good host (see item 211)

First, figure out how many drinks you need (see item 214), and rent some glassware (see item 222).

Check out item 243 for tips on mixing food pairings and item 215 to craft a drink menu.

ANYTHING ELSE?

Disposable cups won't cut it. Then stick to punches (see item 249) and batch everything ahead of time (see item 223).

AFTER DINNER?

Don't forget to offer some food (see item 243) to keep people upright and think about setting the mood (see item 221)

GOT IT. I'M READY.

Um, then maybe you should think about meeting some friends at the park and slinging up some barbecue with a keg.

YES

Think about dessert cocktails (see items 202–210) or serve up some nice spirits neat (see item 271)

THAT SEEMS LIKE TOO MUCH WORK.

214 PLAN YOUR GLASSWARE AND BOOZE

Ending up with leftover booze is never a big problem after a party, but finding yourself with a bunch of random bottles or, worse, a mostly full tapped keg is never good. And just as dreadful is running out of beverages partway through the night. "Oh, look at the time! We should probably head home to, um, water the plants."

When you're planning a party and trying to figure out how much booze to buy, a good standard calculation is 1½ drinks per person per hour, although that number should get lower as the night goes on (or, at least, you hope it does). FYI: A standard keg (15 gallons) will yield about 160 servings. A case of wine is 60 glasses, and each bottle of booze is about 13 shots.

That's a great starting point for a group that's an even mix of big drinkers, teetotalers, and average folks. But you know your friends best, so adjust the numbers upward if you know a lot of party animals, or downward if you've invited a lot of people who need to operate heavy machinery afterward.

215

BUILD A PRO COCKTAIL MENU

➤ The quality of a drink is always important, but the menu it comes from might be even more so. The drinks can illustrate a historical or playful narrative via their names or descriptions, telling a story that entices, educates, and entertains. Bartenders spend a lot of time designing and thinking about menus, but choosing cocktails for a home event isn't hard if you know what to do. Here are a few things to keep in mind.

MAKE IT LEGIBLE Don't spend too much time choosing fonts and flourishes that are completely indecipherable in dim light; choose clean, legible fonts printed at a nice size. Otherwise, you'll spend the rest of the night reading it out loud to everyone.

CHOOSE YOUR DRINKS WISELY If you're planning an event for a large number of people, don't offer drinks that have egg whites or cream, or that involve muddling. Your menu won't be lacking; your guests will be the ones who suffer as they wait for a drink (well, them and your arms). Muddling also produces a giant, wet mess, on top of being slow and exhausting in large numbers. Choose drinks that can be built in glasses, like bucks and mules, old fashioneds, or sparkling wine drinks.

DON'T OVERWHELM YOUR GUESTS Let the size of the space determine how many drinks are manageable. Even in a small bar, offering too many options means that your drinks get lost and people will only order the first few on the list.

KNOW YOUR CLIENTELE You hopefully know your friends well enough to know what theme appeals to them. Are they more likely to drink beer or wine? Offer them your spin on a shandy (see the DST, item 180) or sangria (see item 177). Then you can throw something in there you like and see if you can win them over to other things.

KNOW YOUR SPACE Unless you designed it otherwise, chances are that your house bar isn't built to make a large volume of cocktails. This is why punches are great.

HAVE A RODEO CLOWN OR TWO Just like bull riders need help distracting the animals in order to keep the show going and prevent injuries, you'll need some help keeping the drinks going. Punch is your rodeo clown. They're a great buffer and refilling is easy if you have backup batched punch in the fridge. Put forth a little effort ahead of time to create beautiful garnishes and some signage explaining what's in it, and guests can serve themselves while you get a chance to catch your breath. If you're hosting the party, the last thing you'll want to do is spend your whole time mixing drinks for people.

THINK SEASONALLY No, we aren't going to lecture you about buying local and in season (yes, you should do it), but you should consider the seasons when choosing drinks for your menu. You don't want to put a super boozy old fashioned on there when the humidity levels are sky-high that day. If it's hot out, think refreshing and juicy drinks (it can be as easy as a gin and tonic). If it's cool weather, spirit-focused cocktails are more appropriate.

KNOW THE MAGIC NUMBER If you're hosting a big party, plan for two punches and two cocktails, or one punch if it's no more than 30 people.

VARY THE GLASSWARE Mix up the glassware so you don't have four cocktails that are all in highball glasses, because that's boring. People flock to visually interesting drinks, and using different glasses gives them graphic appeal.

216

COOK UP A HOME BAR

The kitchen may not be the sexiest place, but for most of us, it's simply the best option for a home bar. Here are a few key elements to keep in mind.

WORKSPACE Most kitchens have enough space to move around, plus plenty of surface area to mix at—all at comfortable countertop height (it's important, as stooping can hurt your back). Bonus: Kitchen spaces and their surfaces are designed for easy cleanup.

PLUMBING Probably the most important consideration in a home bar is having access to a sink—you'll need it to rinse equipment and dump out ice. If you set up your bar in a part of the house without plumbing, you'll be constantly running back and forth to the kitchen. You might as well save the effort and just make drinks in there to begin with.

STORAGE Most kitchens are already designed with easy access to storage in mind—including lots of cool, dark spaces for stashing your booze, plus spaces for glassware and equipment. And the kitchen, of course, has the big kahuna: the fridge—where you'll find ice, juices, and syrups galore.

217 | DESIGN A POP-UP BAR

If you're hosting a larger gathering and want to mix cocktails for all your friends, you may need to relocate your bar for the occasion. Keep the same elements in mind–this time in their most mobile applications–and it'll be a painless pop-up party station.

WIGGLE IN A WORKSPACE A folding table works great for temporary setups, but be sure to save your back by adding risers to the legs of the tables. You can use bed risers or simple lengths of PVC pipe to give it a boost–just make sure you choose a wide enough diameter for the legs to fit inside the pipe. Also make sure that you position the tables so that you have room to move around–working smashed up against a wall is not fun.

FIND WATER Try to be in close proximity to a water source and drain. If not, pick up a couple of food-grade buckets at your local hardware store for dumping ice and rinsing bar tools. Put some mats underneath the buckets to keep the floor dry, and a slip-proof gel mat for yourself will also help keep you comfortable.

HIDE THE STOCK Position a tablecloth so that the slack in front completely hides the space underneath the table. This will keep your rinse and dump buckets out of view and allow you to store extras out of sight. If you will be going through a lot of glassware or need different types for different drinks, set up a table behind you to keep them on deck.

HAVE ICE AT THE READY The easiest way to have access to lots of ice is to use a cooler. Stack it on top of milk crates or a spare cooler to bring it up to a comfortable height–about waist height is ideal for scooping.

218 | SET UP YOUR BAR LIKE A PRO

The design of a bar and the placement of the equipment are as crucial for a home bartender as they are for a pro, allowing you to efficiently make drinks and welcome guests at the same time. Before you start stocking, let's explore the space.

→ RAIL Where the most commonly used spirits are kept for popular drinks and special menu items. Ideally, it sits in front of and below the bartender, keeping bottles out of sight but within arm's reach.

Useful at home? A version is helpful for hosting events at home, but feel free to place those most-used bottles on top of the bar. You can also use a row of bottles to hide equipment or recipe cheat sheets.

→ PERSONALITY WELL This station is dedicated to the bartender(s) working to deliver drinks to everyone waiting at the bar, often with personalities as enjoyable as the drinks.

Useful at home? At home, this is your bar and your stage. Be nice to your groupies.

→ UNDERBAR The area underneath the bar for backup bottles of booze, a first-aid kit, towels, and miscellaneous knick-knacks that don't need to be on display.

Useful at home? Yes, and if your bar doesn't have a front to cover the backup bottles of booze and ice, use a tablecloth with all the slack toward the front in order to keep the clutter out of view.

→ BACKBAR The area directly behind the bartender where premium spirits, books, and glassware are kept.

Useful at home? Yes, especially for hosting. If you don't offer a menu, it allows your guests to see what's available, and it keeps your glassware handy.

→ ICE BIN A large stainless-steel tub that sits below or next to a bartender's workstation but above the rail. Professional bins have a clever area for bottles of juice and sparking wine or soda to stay chilled in sleeves.

Useful at home? Yes, because a cocktail without ice is not very far removed from drinking straight out of the bottle. Keep things classy with a large bucket or tub of ice cubes for mixing and filling glasses, along with a smaller container for all your juices, sodas, and mixers.

→ SERVICE WELL If there is more than one bartender, this is the station dedicated to making drinks for the floor (rather than the bar). A bar mat or missing stool in front are your clues to stay out of the way of the waitstaff.

Useful at home? If you're hosting an elegant soirée with passed drinks, setting up a bar in the corner to knock out cocktails is a great idea.

→ BARBACK The person working in unison with the bartender to keep supplies stocked, ensure a clear area and clean equipment, prep juices and garnishes, and do whatever else is needed so that the bartender can focus on making drinks.

Useful at home? If your parties draw large crowds, a barback keeps you mixing and hosting at the same time.

→ GARNISH BIN This compartmentalized tray holds the olives, citrus wedges, cherries, and other garnish items. If you aren't the one bartending, don't touch it—and definitely don't help yourself to its contents.

Useful at home? It can be, but it's not necessary. A few nice glasses or small bowls will work; just don't forget the garnish tongs.

USBG | ST. LOUIS CHAPTER

✦ **MATT SORRELL** ✦

Co-owner | Cocktails Are Go!

219

GO WITH THE FLOW

The location of your home bar for entertaining is as important as the drinks themselves. Of particular significance is the flow of the space—good to consider for any event and critical for large ones—even if it's a self-serve bar.

People will naturally migrate to the booze and to each other, which means you should think about where those clusters will form and their effect on the party's foot traffic. Try to position the bar in a room that has multiple points of entry and provides exits to other rooms, so people can come and go and not create a logjam in front of the bar. Avoid rooms with dead ends, like porches or sunrooms, which give folks nowhere to go once they've got a drink in hand.

220 ⟡ MAKE EYE CONTACT

➻ If the space allows, try to position the bar setup in a way that will allow you to make eye contact with guests when they enter, especially if the host will be mixing the drinks. It makes people feel welcome and lets them know where the host is—and, most important, where to get their booze.

221 { SET THE MOOD }

People go to parties for the same reason they go to bars (and no, it's not just to drink): to socialize and connect with each other. A good party atmosphere, like a great bar, encourages that to happen.

•➻ **COMFORT** Everyday seating arrangements don't always work for larger gatherings. Make sure seats don't block doors or isolate people, and aren't too far from surfaces to rest plates and drinks. A few kiosk tables spread throughout the party and some extra chairs will make everyone more comfortable.

•➻ **LIGHTING** Nothing is more intimidating than a bright light straight in the face, making you feel like you're sitting in an interrogation room. Dim the lights, or, if that's not possible, swap out the bulbs for something with a lower wattage and a warmer glow. You can also keep them off completely and instead use lamps or portable shop lights covered with lighting gels.

•➻ **TUNES** The volume and type of music you choose will also have an effect on the party. Here you need to know your guests and theme, and choose appropriately, keeping tabs on the volume as people come and go. Chances are great you'll find something suitable on a music streaming service if you don't feel like building a playlist.

222 | DON'T DO THE DISHES

So you start planning your party and then get a little panicky when you realize that you want to serve martinis to 50 people but you don't have the glassware. Don't switch to plastic—there's a simple and elegant solution: Rent them from a local events or party-supply company.

Depending on the size of your order, you may need to pick them up yourself if you don't meet the minimum (though if you need extra linens, tables, and seats, your event is probably big enough). If you are having the event catered, you can often have the catering company supply the goods, as they often get regular deliveries of event rentals.

The best part? They arrive clean and, once you're done, you get to send them back without having to wash a single one.

223

BATCH A PLAN

You can batch pretty much any cocktail in advance and then either shake or stir as you need them, but there are a few considerations you'll want to keep in mind.

Cocktails that contain egg whites or cream are bad ideas at a giant event, because you can't batch them ahead of time. They need a good amount of shaking to build the volume and texture they're known for, and, like French fries, need to be consumed immediately after making them.

If your drink calls for anything with bubbles in it, keep everything as cold as possible (the bubbles will last longer that way), and only add the sparkling component at the very end—to each individual drink.

224

SCALE YOUR RECIPE BY RATIOS

This is a good time to break out your spreadsheet application to do all the hard math for you. If that's not your thing, rethink a recipe as ratios. There will always be anomalies, but for the most part you can simply break them down in parts. For example, the basic sour recipe (see item 046) is 2 ounces spirit to ¾ ounce each citrus and sweetener, which may not be an elegant and easy number, but it can also be thought of as the 8:3:3 ratio. Messy, yes, but easier in a pinch.

225

MIX THE BUCKET

⤻ Unless you have access to a commercial kitchen space, chances are you don't have huge containers lying around in which to mix up and store large amounts of batched cocktails. But your local big-box hardware store (yes, hardware store) probably has the solution: inexpensive 5-gallon (19-liter) food-grade plastic buckets. You can get a bucket and lid for fairly cheap (and you can also opt for just the bucket, depending on your needs). Make sure it's food-grade, and not just for mixing paint, and then all you'll need is more room in the fridge.

226 | PRE-BATCH YOUR DRINKS

⤻ Sometimes you don't need to batch a whole cocktail ahead of time, either because you want to maintain a little bit of showmanship or you're just looking to turn a six-ingredient drink into an easy two-parter. Pre-batching is another popular way to offer good-quality but speedy cocktails. The idea is that you combine all of the nonvolatile ingredients together, such as spirits, liqueurs, sweeteners, and syrups. But make sure you start by making one cocktail, taking note of the total volume of nonvolatile ingredients you need per drink. Then when pouring from the batch, measure carefully. Don't eyeball it or your drink will be off-balance.

227 | GIVE A WARM WELCOME AND A COLD DRINK

⟩⟩→ Don't let the excitement of mixing drinks for your friends turn you into a source of the bottleneck at your own party. If you say hi to everyone and mix each individual drink, you'll wind up with a line. Unless you have a TSA theme, don't make your friends wait 40 minutes for a drink. Here's how to avoid the wait times.

Plan on pre-batching the first and last drink, if serving more than two—it will free up your hands and provide more time for up-front socializing and introductions. Make sure you greet everyone and offer a welcome with one of your pre-batched cocktails, and set out a self-serve station with a punch bowl, pitchers, bottled cocktails, or Jell-O shots so that guests can help themselves right away, even if they're not interested in the go-to cocktail option. This will give you more time for last-minute preparations (no matter how much planning you do, you're bound to forget something).

If you really want to shake individual drinks as people arrive, mix up the classics ahead of time with everything except ice, garnishes, or sodas, then simply shake and serve.

228

HAVE FUN WITH ICE MOLDS

Making your own ice is an easy way to add an extra touch of fun by freezing citrus, herbs, flowers, and other garnishes into the block.

Because most homemade ice comes out slightly cloudy, your decorative elements should be on the bottom or top of the mold. Using ice molds or a plain old ice tray, layer your garnishes on the bottom, add a tiny bit of water, freeze, add more water, freeze again. You can continue adding garnishes in layers as you like, stopping with the topmost portion about three-quarters of the way so that a layer of ice can form above it.

SLICE AND DICE YOUR ICE

229

Truly clear ice requires breaking down large blocks sourced from ice companies. An ice saw will set you back a couple hundred dollars, so it's not really for the hobbyist bartender—stick to molds at home, or order cut ice from local ice sculptors (see item 040). But the process of breaking down a 300-pound (136-kg) block of ice into smaller serving sizes is good to be aware of.

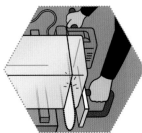 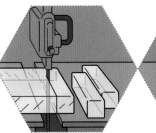 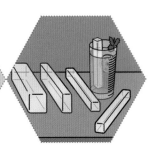

STEP ONE An electric chainsaw with a milling attachment (set to the appropriate thickness) is used to cut manageable-size planks of ice from the big block. The thickness will determine the size of the resulting cubes.

STEP TWO A band (or the chainsaw) is used to cut the slabs into columns, making them as uniform as possible, equal in width and height.

STEP THREE Those columns are then cut into cubes.

STEP FOUR To make ice spears for Collins and highball drinks, the slab is cut into smaller slabs, about half the size of the columns, then cut again in half lengthwise into long spears.

230

DON'T GET STUCK

After all the hard work that goes into cutting up your ice, don't let your cubes or spears stick to each other in the freezer. The simple solution is vodka. No, not for you (especially not if the chainsaw is still around), but for the ice.

Using a clean spray bottle filled with vodka, mist your ice with a thin layer on all sides. The lower freezing temperature of the vodka will keep the cubes from sticking to each other.

232

CRAFT DELICIOUSLY POTABLE WATER

➤ One of the most commonly overlooked critical elements of a party is water. Water keeps everybody hydrated (important in avoiding hangovers), and also slows down the speed at which people drink. A little effort in making water accessible and delicious only makes the party better.

You can use the peels of citrus, stray mint leaves, cucumber rind, and garnish scraps to create a delicious, spa-style water infusion for your guests. This is a low-effort way to make water appealing, while also reducing bar waste and efficiently using the entire product. Adding some hero citrus wheels and cucumber slices keeps it looking pretty and delicious.

231

SALUTE THOSE ABOUT TO MOCK(TAIL)

➤ Having a couple of mocktails up your sleeve is a useful hospitality tool. Your guests may be asking for them for any number of reasons, but ultimately they're looking for a way to enjoy the occasion, avoid feeling left out, or sidestep anyone around them who might feel uncomfortable with a nondrinker in their midst. And keep in mind that the reason a guest isn't drinking is probably none of your business; a new diet, medication interactions, early pregnancy, or a hop on the wagon are all possibilities—as is "I'm still hungover from last night, man."

The look and feel of a mocktail is just as important as the taste, and if the drink doesn't give off that party vibe, it defeats a large part of the effort. So from garnish to glassware, make sure your guest doesn't feel as though he's sitting at the kids' table.

Here are some basic rules for crafting a good mocktail. They should be dry, balanced, and delicious—just like all your recipes.

DO

•➧ Keep them dry; the pucker prevents guests from drinking them too quickly and can offer the slight shudder of a spiked drink.

•➧ Approach a mocktail the same way you would a cocktail: keeping balance, dilution, and flavor in mind.

•➧ Build drinks in Collins or highballs, since it doesn't matter if they've got more volume.

•➧ Start with the flavors you have at your disposal by looking at your juices, syrups, and bitters.

•➧ Keep the formulas of sours and palomas in mind as you develop a recipe.

DON'T

•➧ Beware falling into the "virgin" trap— simply removing the liquor from an enjoyable cocktail won't make for a good drink.

•➧ Putting sparkling water on ice does not a mocktail make—give your guests something worth bragging about.

•➧ Don't use teeny-weeny glassware, no matter how pretty. Mocktails are easier to drink, and will need a refill in seconds flat.

•➧ Avoid using up all your bar prep (mixers, syrups, etc.) too quickly. You'll need them for the cocktails, too!

•➧ Don't lean too heavily on juices or syrups. Use plenty of soda water, tonic, and ginger beer so it doesn't get too sugary.

234

MOCK THEIR SOCKS OFF

Using cocktail bitters in mocktails is controversial, since they are typically alcoholic—but they are used in such small quantities that they end up contributing just trace amounts. Bitters are great for adding layers of complexity to an otherwise simple (and alcohol-free) drink. Just make sure that your guest isn't allergic or completely opposed to the idea. Here are a few great recipe ideas for the zero-proof crowd.

235 | SAINT TIKI

2 oz orange juice

2 oz pineapple juice

¾ oz lime juice

½ oz cinnamon simple syrup (1:1)

2 dashes Tiki bitters (optional)

Ginger beer

Mint sprig to garnish

→ *Combine orange, pineapple, and lime juices, cinnamon syrup, and bitters (if using) in a cocktail shaker. Add ice, shake hard 8–10 seconds, and strain into a cold coupe or cocktail glass. Top with ginger beer and garnish with a mint sprig.*

236 { FAUX-LOMA }

2 oz grapefruit juice

1 oz lime juice

1 oz simple syrup (1:1)

Soda water or grapefruit soda

Lime wedge to garnish

→ *Combine grapefruit juice, lime juice, and simple syrup in a cocktail shaker. Add ice, shake hard 8–10 seconds, and strain into a Collins or highball glass with ice. Top with soda water (or grapefruit soda, if using) and garnish with a lime wedge.*

237

HONEYBEE FIZZ

2 oz lemon juice

1½ oz rich honey syrup (2:1)

Soda water

2 dashes Angostura bitters (optional)

Cherry to garnish

→ *In a Collins or highball glass with ice, add the lemon juice and honey syrup and stir. Top with soda water. Add bitters and garnish with a cherry.*

238

WILD MULE

1 oz lime juice

½ oz simple syrup (1:1)

Ginger beer

Lime wheel to garnish

In a copper mug or old-fashioned glass with ice, add the lime juice and simple syrup. Top with ginger beer and garnish with a lime wheel.

239 | WATERMELON-GINGER GELATIN SHOTS

It's hard not to find cocktail Jell-O shots fun, and they're even better when they're made inside a hollowed-out piece of fruit. Make sure that the liquid tastes sweeter than you would normally like, since the sweetness will settle down once the gelatin sets. Here's a recipe that uses small watermelons, but you can use any fruit with a rind.

1 watermelon (small)	4 oz cold water
½ cup lemonade	2 tablespoons powdered gelatin (1 envelope)
1 cup watermelon juice	
1 cup ginger liqueur	6 oz boiling water
½ cup Lillet rosé aperitif	Hibiscus sea salt (or any flaky salt) to finish

•➧ *Cut the watermelon in half and scoop out the flesh (you can use this to make the juice). Cut a small slice off the bottom of each half to create a stable base—you don't want them spilling in your fridge.*

•➧ *In a separate bowl, combine the lemonade, watermelon juice, liqueur, and aperitif, and set aside.*

•➧ *In a heatproof container, add the cold water to the powdered gelatin, and stir to combine. Then add the boiling water and stir until the gelatin completely dissolves. Add the cocktail mixture and stir until well mixed. Pour the whole thing into the hollowed-out watermelons and refrigerate overnight.*

•➧ *Once the liquid has set, you can slice the melon, sprinkling each "watermelon slice" with a small pinch of salt. Serve with a spoon. Makes 24 servings.*

240 | HAVE NO BONES ABOUT IT

Gelatin is an animal-based product, made from the collagen extracted from byproducts (like bones and skin) of meat production. For many people, such as vegetarians, vegans, and those on restricted diets for religious reasons, gelatin isn't something they can eat. Thankfully, there are plant-based substitutes like agar-agar, which can do the same job as gelatin. Just be aware that the texture will be firmer and a bit more crumbly. To use agar-agar in any gelatin recipes, simply substitute 1 teaspoon powdered agar-agar for every tablespoon of gelatin, and heat up the agar-agar along with the hot water.

241

FEAR THE EDIBLE SHOT

I'll be honest: Of all the ways to enjoy a cocktail, none of them scare me more than the edible gelatin cocktail. While the effects of a standard cocktail are usually quickly apparent, gelatin shots lead to a delayed reaction that can be much harder to anticipate—especially if you indulge in too many, thinking you don't feel the effects. You will, soon, and you might find yourself suddenly sideways. Be smart, and don't have more than two in any given evening.

242 { GROW SOME BOURBON BALLS }

Letting these confections rest is key to getting the best flavor, but be careful not to wait too long to eat them—they will start to fall apart as the whiskey evaporates out of the pastry. If whiskey isn't your thing, this recipe also works with any spirit of your choice.

1 box (12 oz) vanilla wafers, broken into pieces

6 oz semisweet chocolate, finely chopped

½ cup (3½ oz) firmly packed light brown sugar

¼ cup (2½ oz) light corn syrup

3 oz bourbon whiskey

Pinch of salt

2 cups (8 oz) pecans, lightly toasted and finely chopped

Place the vanilla wafer pieces into a heavy-duty zip-top bag and give them a few whacks with a rolling pin, crushing finely. Melt the chocolate in a double boiler over simmering water, stirring occasionally. Transfer to a bowl and add the brown sugar, corn syrup, bourbon, and salt. Stir until completely blended and then mix in the crushed wafers and half of the pecans.

Shape the dough into 1-inch (2.5-cm) balls and spread the remaining pecans on a plate. Roll the balls to coat evenly.

Use wax paper between layers to store the bourbon balls in a tightly covered container. Keep in the fridge for 24 hours before serving to allow the flavors to blend. Makes about 4 dozen.

KATE BOLTON ✦ Bar Manager | Americano

243 | PLAY MATCHMAKER WITH DRINKS AND DINNER

➤→ Finding foods that work well with cocktails isn't always easy, mostly due to the more powerful flavors and alcohol content that can crush any delicate or subtle ingredients. But it is possible and even a preferred way to enjoy a drink. Here are a few things to try at your next gathering.

THINK BEYOND TRADITIONAL BAR FLAVORS
Incorporate foods like pistachio, grain mustard, and hops, as well as spices like long pepper or pink peppercorn into your cocktails as infusions, tinctures, or syrups. Do not be afraid to apply culinary techniques to achieve fresh and exciting pairings, such as making absinthe into a sorbet, grilling strawberries before turning them into a syrup, or infusing cognac with brown butter.

AVOID OVERUSING INGREDIENTS A handful of ingredients go with absolutely everything across the food and drink spectrum—such as ginger, almond, lemon, anise, and black pepper. But using these flavors in every drink or dish gets boring quickly. Try to find different ways to coax out similar flavors. Use fennel or Thai basil instead of absinthe, or make a hazelnut syrup instead of using the standard almond orgeat.

DON'T DUPLICATE FOOD FLAVORS Like putting together an outfit, choose complementary rather than matching. If a dish has rosemary, try to use an herb like thyme in the accompanying cocktail. And if you're serving something tomato heavy, use strawberries in your drinks—the chemical compounds and flavor profiles of tomatoes and strawberries are actually quite similar, so their natural affinity for each other make for a great pairing without becoming identical flavor twins.

BUILD COCKTAIL PAIRINGS A good rule of thumb is to think about your cocktail choice the same way you would think about wine. If you will be serving light seafood, make a lighter-style drink that has higher acidity and some effervescence, such as a sparkling wine cocktail or a daiquiri. Whereas if you're having something meaty and braised, you might want something richer and darker, like a Manhattan. Just be careful with the boozy drinks—if it's too high in alcohol, it will overpower the dish.

SAVE ROOM FOR DESSERT If you plan on pairing drinks with dessert, the cocktail choice should be sweeter than whatever the dessert is. Otherwise the cocktail will taste washed-out and flavorless next to its sweet counterpart.

244

AVOID MAKING A MEAL OUT OF COCKTAILS

In many cultures, drinking always comes with food. The Japanese have the *izakaya*, Spanish the tapas bars, and Koreans the *hof* or *sul-jip*. Drinks and bites are designed to be enjoyed together—and trust us, the story of when fried chicken met soju is a heartwarming tale of true love. In Mexican cantinas, *botanas* (or snacks) will often accompany drinks, getting progressively bigger and heartier with each drink order. In Italy, the aperitivo hour usually includes olives, chips, and other snacks to enjoy with a spritz or other aperitif drinks. Bitter flavors and fatty foods work deliciously well together.

The mythical three-martini lunch (or dinner) is considered a badge of honor in some circles, but that's a recipe made by stirring up trouble and garnishing it with a string of bad decisions—not to mention an unspeakable hangover. If you're going to drink, don't do it on an empty stomach.

245

PREPARE TO LAYER

Not all garnishes need to sit at the edge of the glass or on top of the drink. Drinks with ice—and long drinks in particular—can be decorated with herbs or thin slices of fruits or vegetables used as layers in between the ice and along the side of the glass.

Before you start, make sure you have your garnishes ready: herbs, berries, thinly sliced cucumber or citrus rounds, apple slices, or anything else you want to use. Using your garnish tongs, arrange your garnishes in the glass, add ice, and continue to build up until your glass is filled. Just be sure to not overload it or your drink won't fit!

USBG | SAN FRANCISCO CHAPTER ✦ **JENNIFER COLLIAU** ✦ Owner of Small Hand Foods

246 { MAKE YOUR DRINK AS COLD AS A POLAR BEAR'S GLASS }

You'll notice that a spirit-forward drink or neat pours of spirits at nicer bars will sometimes come served with spherical or large ice cube (often barely fitting in the glass). This minimizes the surface area that the liquid comes in contact with, thereby decreasing the rate of dilution. A bunch of small ice cubes has the most surface area, and a single sphere has the least—well, almost. Why "almost"? Because freezing a layer of water directly into your glass will give you a single plane with the least amount of surface area and dilution. Just make sure your glassware is tempered before you stick it in the freezer.

247

LAYER YOUR DRINK WITH ARSENIC AND LACE

In some cases, you can also layer your cocktails. The trick is to work with liquids that have different specific gravities so that layers will stay happily in equilibrium. The general gist is that higher-proof liquors will float, while sweeter liqueurs will sink.

This interpretation of the classic 1940s Arsenic & Lace drink, most likely named after the popular play (and movie adaptation) *Arsenic and Old Lace* by Joseph Kesserling, tells a story as you drink. Opening with the drama of heavy anise notes and a hint of citrus, things soften up with the botanicals of the gin and vermouth, and it ends in classic Hollywood fashion: sweet and floral.

½ oz absinthe

1½ oz gin (one with milder juniper flavor preferred)

1½ oz dry vermouth

2 dashes orange bitters

½ oz crème de violette

•➜ STEP ONE Add the absinthe to a glass with ice and stir to *louche* (a French term for the clouding of the absinthe—a result of the aromatic oils separating out due to the addition of water from the ice). Set aside; this will be your "lace" garnish.

•➜ STEP TWO In a mixing glass with ice, combine the gin, vermouth, and bitters. Stir 20-30 seconds, until well chilled. Strain the cocktail into a small white wine glass.

•➜ STEP THREE Measure out the crème de violette in a small measuring cup. Place a barspoon, with the convex side facing up, so it touches the inside of the glass, and slowly pour the crème de violette so it slides down the glass and accumulates at the bottom. This pool of crème de violette is your "arsenic."

•➜ STEP FOUR Insert a straw into the absinthe, placing the pad of your finger over the opening to draw it up. With the loaded straw over the drink, remove your finger to release the absinthe and watch it lace the top half of the glass. Repeat until most of the absinthe has been used. A large eyedropper can be used in place of the straw, but don't be too gentle—you want the force of the liquid to break the surface.

DRINK AROUND THE WORLD

➤ Many countries across the globe are known for specific cocktails; some have traveled far and wide while others may remain close to their place of origin. Here are a few traditional drinks you might encounter during your travels.

CANADA
A Canadian favorite is the Caesar, which might remind some of a Bloody Mary (see item 183). The Caesar is made with vodka, Clamato (clam juice), hot sauce, celery, and lime.

MEXICO
The Paloma is a tequila specialty, made with grapefruit juice, soda, lemon, and simple syrup.

CUBA The Mojito, of course (see item 165).

NICARAGUA
The national drink of Nicaragua is *El Macuá*, named for the tropical bird. The cocktail is made with rum, guava and lemon juices, and simple syrup.

ECUADOR
The *Canelazo* is a hot drink made with fruit juices, cinnamon sticks, brown sugar, water, and rum. It's a traditional Christmastime beverage.

BRAZIL The national drink of Brazil is the *Caipirinha*: lime, sugar, and cachaça (see item 115).

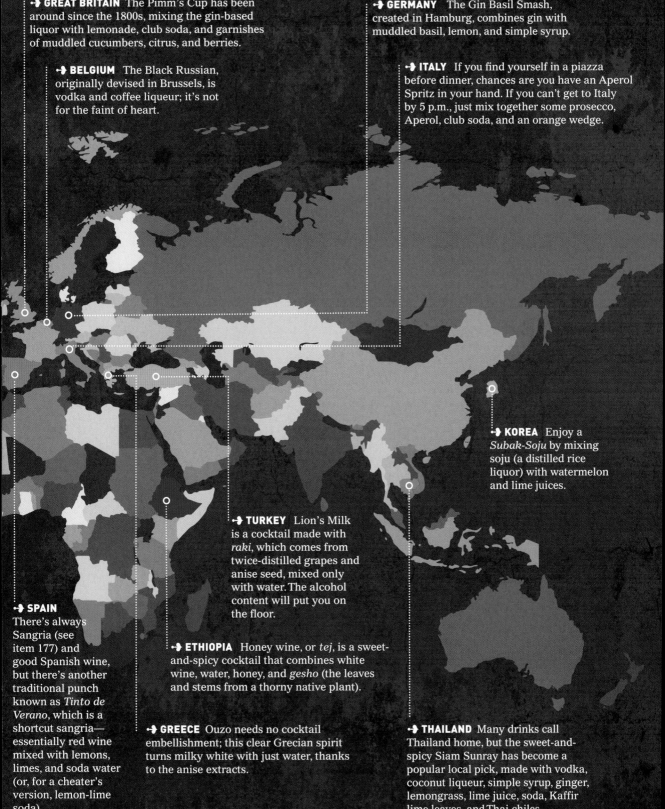

GREAT BRITAIN The Pimm's Cup has been around since the 1800s, mixing the gin-based liquor with lemonade, club soda, and garnishes of muddled cucumbers, citrus, and berries.

BELGIUM The Black Russian, originally devised in Brussels, is vodka and coffee liqueur; it's not for the faint of heart.

GERMANY The Gin Basil Smash, created in Hamburg, combines gin with muddled basil, lemon, and simple syrup.

ITALY If you find yourself in a piazza before dinner, chances are you have an Aperol Spritz in your hand. If you can't get to Italy by 5 p.m., just mix together some prosecco, Aperol, club soda, and an orange wedge.

KOREA Enjoy a *Subak-Soju* by mixing soju (a distilled rice liquor) with watermelon and lime juices.

TURKEY Lion's Milk is a cocktail made with *raki*, which comes from twice-distilled grapes and anise seed, mixed only with water. The alcohol content will put you on the floor.

SPAIN There's always Sangria (see item 177) and good Spanish wine, but there's another traditional punch known as *Tinto de Verano*, which is a shortcut sangria—essentially red wine mixed with lemons, limes, and soda water (or, for a cheater's version, lemon-lime soda).

ETHIOPIA Honey wine, or *tej*, is a sweet-and-spicy cocktail that combines white wine, water, honey, and *gesho* (the leaves and stems from a thorny native plant).

GREECE Ouzo needs no cocktail embellishment; this clear Grecian spirit turns milky white with just water, thanks to the anise extracts.

THAILAND Many drinks call Thailand home, but the sweet-and-spicy Siam Sunray has become a popular local pick, made with vodka, coconut liqueur, simple syrup, ginger, lemongrass, lime juice, soda, Kaffir lime leaves, and Thai chiles.

249

PARTY WITH PUNCH

Punches are some of the oldest and most classic of drinks. They are the entertainer's workhorse, all about sharing and socializing. Make a punch and prepare for a lingering, long afternoon or evening filled with conversation.

Punch comes from the Sanskrit word *pañc*, the number five. Traditionally, a punch has five basic ingredients: some kind of liquor, citrus, a sweetener, water, and tea or spices. The drink as we know it is thought to have evolved from the tradition of wassailing, when a hot cider or wine mulled beverage was enjoyed in a ceremony to ensure a good harvest.

250

FISH HOUSE PUNCH

This recipe is based on the 1732 version first concocted in Philadelphia at the Schuylkill Fishing Company, a fishing club colloquially known as the "Fish House."

3 ½ cups water

1 cup sugar

1½ cups fresh lemon juice (6–8 lemons), strained

One 750-ml bottle Jamaican amber rum

12 oz cognac

2 oz peach brandy

8 lemon slices to garnish

In a large bowl that fits in your refrigerator, combine water and sugar until dissolved. Add the lemon juice, rum, cognac, and brandy, and mix. Cover, then chill. When ready to serve, place a block of ice in a serving bowl, add punch, and lemon slices.

251

MAKE OLEO SACCHARUM

Despite its scientific-sounding name, oleo saccharum is nothing more than a citrus-sugar syrup made by mixing sugar with citrus peels. Using the lemon peels in addition to the juice to flavor the punch will add a richness and brightness you can't get any other way.

Make your own concentrated lemon syrup by peeling seven lemons with a vegetable peeler and combining the peels with about a cup of sugar. Mash it gently with a muddler and then throw it all into a zip-top bag for a few hours until the sugar dissolves, extracting the citrus oils.

252 { BREW SOME TEA SYRUP }

Thanks to its tannins, tea can add a nice extra dimension to a punch, while also providing an alternative method for getting fragrant citrus oils out of the fruit peels and into the drinks. Adapt your favorite punch recipe to incorporate just a few modifications in order to subtly change the flavors.

Heat the amount of water called for in your punch recipe until it comes to a simmer. Remove from the heat and add Earl Grey tea, the peels from the lemons, and the sugar as directed in the original recipe. Stir to combine, cover, and let cool.

Once cool, combine with the remaining ingredients in your punch recipe and enjoy!

253 | FESTOON YOUR DRINKS

For the most part, garnishes don't require any specialty tools beyond what you most likely already have in your kitchen. A sharp vegetable peeler, a paring knife, and a zester are all you really need. If you want to get fancier, you could invest in a channeling knife to make finer twists. Here are some garnishes to get you started.

SUGAR-DUSTED MINT SPRIGS
Mint leaves dusted in powdered sugar make for a striking garnish on any mint-flavored cocktails—and it's especially jolly around the holidays.

CUCUMBER ROSES
Turn a long, thin cucumber slice into a rosette, or coil loosely to line the inside of a glass.

PEEL ROSES
See item 255.

WEDGES
Cut the fruit from stem to blossom end and make a shallow slit for positioning on the rim of the glass.

SERRATED TWISTS
Give your twists some pizzazz by using decorative scissors to give them zig-zag or scalloped edges.

CITRUS WHEELS
Starting at the blossom or stem end, simply cut slices. A mandolin will allow you to make very thin slices.

CITRUS TWISTS
See item 256.

FLAGS
Cut a twist, then place a cherry inside (or next to) the peel, and spear with a cocktail pick.

254 | GARNISH LIKE A PRO

Categorically speaking, a garnish is a flourish added to a cocktail to make it as visually appealing as it is delicious. Sweet or salty rims on the glass, verdant herbs, aromatic peels, briny pickled vegetables, fragrant flowers, or candied fruits all add a complementary flavor element. But even items like specialty plastic or metal straws, paper parasols, or specialty glassware can be considered a garnish—as they all let your eyes drink first.

The popularity of garnishes is said to have exploded during Prohibition, particularly to mask cheap, poorly made booze or watered-down drinks. But for many of today's bartenders, garnishing has become as much an element of personal expression as the recipes themselves, with social media adding extra pressure to give the drink visual distinction.

But before you leap into designing elaborate garnishes for your drinks, let's learn some basics.

255

GET A ROSY OUTLOOK

Cutting a rose garnish is simpler than it seems. Start with a long peel from a citrus fruit, and wind the peel around itself, using your index finger as a spool to tighten. Then turn the wound peel over and remove your finger while pinching the peel together. Spear with a cocktail pick.

DO THE TWIST

256

Most garnishes can be prepared a day in advance and stored in the fridge. Wrap herbs in a damp paper towel before storing in an airtight container.

TWIST A twist of citrus is basic and versatile—and once you get the hang of it, you'll be doing them in your sleep.

STEP ONE With one hand gripping the fruit, start peeling from the stem end, moving vertically toward the blossom end. Use gentle pressure so you aren't digging into the skin too much. Let the tool do the work.

STEP TWO As you're moving the peeler down, use the index and middle finger of your gripping hand to secure the top portion of the peel as you continue to cut the bottom half.

LONG TWIST Garnishes that require more fruit can be difficult for beginners, as getting one long swath of citrus can be challenging. Find a peeler you feel most comfortable with and let the tool do the work.

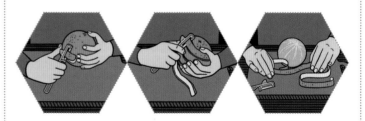

STEP ONE Hold the fruit so that you can rotate it via an imaginary axis that runs from blossom to stem end.

STEP TWO Starting at the bottom, rotate the citrus as you run the peeler around it, holding the cut peel as you turn. Guide the peeler as it cuts upward, until you reach the top of the fruit.

STEP THREE The long peel, called a horse's neck, can be coiled inside a glass.

257 | TAKE WING

A wing garnish takes a bit more work, but it makes for a spectacular presentation.

•→ STEP ONE Peel a long 4-inch (10-cm) peel from a citrus fruit.

•→ STEP TWO Trim the edges, cut the short ends diagonally, and make a lengthwise cut in the middle.

•→ STEP THREE Make small slits around the diagonal end of the peel (these will be the feathers of the wings).

•→ STEP FOUR Tightly roll the peel on itself and place the garnish on a glass using the middle slit.

VODKA

IF YOU EVER WANT TO STIR THE NATIONALISM OF A POLE AND RUSSIAN SITTING IN THE SAME ROOM, ASK THEM WHO INVENTED VODKA.

258

GET THE HISTORY

➤→ Historical proof is absent when it comes to vodka's country of origin, and with both Poland and Russia producing it longer than anyone else, it's just safest to know your audience and declare one, the other, or both as the correct answer.

One thing is for sure: The 18th century saw industrial production in both countries, followed by state-controlled production soon after. By the turn of the 20th century, the average Russian, due to a combination of state production and national encouragement, was drinking a staggering (and stumbling) average of 29 gallons (110 liters) of vodka a year. That's about a bottle every 2½ days—per person.

The combination of the October Revolution and World War II saw distillers flee to begin production in other parts of the world, such as Paris, Istanbul, and even New York. In the United States, vodka was initially sold as white whiskey, and it wasn't until 1962—when James Bond ordered a vodka martini in *Dr. No*—that vodka came into demand.

While it's polite to withhold judgment on anyone's drink of choice, I believe you can always do better than Mr. Bond's shaken vodka martini—even the Vesper (see item 104), which isn't too far from the formula, is still about 100 times better when it comes to vodka cocktails.

259

REDISCOVER VODKA'S USES

There are plenty of people who think that vodka is a waste of time. "Why bother with vodka when I can drink something with flavor?" is the refrain. That may be true in some cases, but vodka has plenty of promise. One of its best uses is when the flavor of the base spirit is too concentrated, as with an intense gin that can be mellowed with a partial substitution of vodka. Vodka's neutral flavor also works well when there's already enough going on in a recipe; sometimes you just want to focus on flavors other than liquor, like the pristine citrus from your backyard tree or the amazing produce you picked up from the farmers' market. And of course, vodka is also great for infusing (see item 034). Spices, herbs, teas, and fruit can all be used in combination with vodka in order to add a bright punch of unusual flavor.

Vodka can be made from many base ingredients, including potatoes, beets, and grains, but the process remains the same for all.

STEP ONE The base goes through the fermentation process. Since vodka can be made from almost any food that will ferment, this step varies according to the ingredient being used and how it is fermented.

STEP TWO Continuous-column stills, which strip out safe and good-tasting alcohols in one pass, are usually used. Often the number of distillations is bragged about on the bottle, but it's usually meaningless. The number of times distilled is less important than how well the vodka is made.

STEP THREE Dilution of a spirit is important (for taste, and also for legal reasons), but not as critical as it is with vodka, since about half of what's in the bottle is water added after distillation. Just like water in different places tastes different, good-tasting water makes good-tasting vodka.

STEP FOUR Most spirits are filtered, but filtration methods have become a selling point in a crowded market. Cellulose and freeze- or chill-filtering are necessary, and charcoal is fine for flavorless vodka. Filtering through diamonds, lava, or four-leaf clovers isn't going to do anything except make it cost more.

261

DEFINE VODKA

➤➤ Unlike other spirits, vodka is not defined by what it's made of, but rather by the process by which it is distilled.

This means you can make vodka out of basically anything that can be fermented—such as fruits, vegetables, grains, sugarcane, potatoes, sugar beets, honey, molasses, and even milk or maple syrup. The list goes on.

In order for vodka to become vodka, it must be distilled to at least 190 proof (90 percent ABV), although once it reaches 96 percent ABV it becomes something called an azeotrope, wherein further concentration isn't possible by distillation.

Does this mean you can taste the base ingredients in the final product? Amazingly, yes, although often in incredibly subtle ways—and usually only if you're drinking it at room temperature out of a wine glass (and rarely in cocktails).

And yes, all vodka, no matter its base, filtration method, or distillation process, will give you a hangover.

262 SET YOUR DRINK AFLAME

▶→ Blame it on the showmanship nature that an audience creates: The bar is a stage for mixing cocktails, and all cocktail roads eventually lead to fire. It always impresses, whether as a final flourish or just simply setting the whole damn drink ablaze.

Safety first, however: Mixing fire with drinking is not, to put it mildly, recommended under any circumstance, especially when there's no fire extinguisher or designated driver to haul you to the emergency room if your confidence overwhelms your abilities. If you insist on playing with fire, keep the following rules in mind: Never drink alone, make sure you have an extinguisher handy, and do your mixing in the kitchen, far away from anything flammable.

If things get too hot, remember: Stop, drop, and roll.

263

FLOAT A TIKI TORCH GARNISH

▶→ Drinks in bowls and fire as a garnish are both common in tiki bars, and one easy way to get the effect is by using the spent half of a lime or lemon on your latest tiki cocktail.

Grab a lime or lemon that's leftover from hand squeezing and float it in the bowl (a punch with multiple straws is ideal). Make sure it's steady, and then add a crouton soaked in lemon oil to the floating raft.

Then urge your audience to stand back—and light it up!

264

FLAME AN ORANGE PEEL

The most common and relatively safe—yet still quite dramatic—way to add a little fire to your cocktails is by flaming an orange peel over a drink. This caramelizes the citrus oils and also creates a sudden flash of fire that keeps things interesting.

•➜ **STEP ONE** Using a paring knife, cut a circle of peel from an unwaxed orange. Hold it between the thumb and forefinger of your dominant hand, zest side toward the drink. Light a match and position it about 4 inches (10 cm) from the drink.

•➜ **STEP TWO** Pinch the zest quickly so that the oils in the skin jet toward the match and cocktail.

•➜ **STEP THREE** Moisten the rim of the glass with the orange peel. Note: If you end up with a sooty peel, it means that your orange is waxed. Avoid using waxed fruit as it will contribute a sooty-chemical flavor.

•➜ **STEP FOUR** Garnish your drink with the flamed peel and enjoy!

265 { USE A RED-HOT POKER }

➤➜ Using fire in drinks has been a practice since the 19th century, when taverns would offer hot drinks in mugs heated with a red-hot iron kept in the fireplace. Called loggerheads, the iron would be plunged into a mug to make a toddy or flip (consisting of an egg, beer, spirit, and sweetener). You can see a modern version at Booker & Dax in New York's Lower East Side, where a custom-built poker makes for dramatically heated drinks.

The benefit of this method is the caramelization that occurs when the red-hot metal comes in contact with the drink; the biggest challenge is finding a food-grade piece of iron (or another heating element) to use. Once you've got that covered, simply mix up the Hot English Rum Flip (see item 195) in a heatproof pitcher, place the hot metal into the drink, and watch it froth—or "flip," which is how the drink style got its name.

266 ADD SOME FLAIR, BARTENDER

Bartending isn't only about making tasty drinks; it's also about entertaining your guests with a few well-timed flicks and throws. Some tricks require a lot of practice, especially the bottle throws, and most require at least some time rehearsing to get the timing down. Practice with empty bottles first, then try them with water to get used to the weight (and spillable nature) of open liquor bottles.

267 LEARN THE BOTTLE STALL

Here are a few basic flair techniques from Dario Doimo—a winner of more than 50 flair bartending competitions, USBG National Flair Champion two years in a row, and a performer of flair bartending in more than 20 countries. Let's start with the bottle stall.

•➧ STEP ONE
Use your dominant hand to pick up the bottle by its neck with three fingers (index, middle, and thumb) and move it straight up into the air, careful not to flip the bottle. You want the bottle to simply travel up and down.

•➧ STEP TWO
With a loose hand, fingers lightly spread, catch the bottom of the bottle with the back of your hand, so that it lands with knuckles in the center of the bottle. Take care to move your hand with the bottle's motion and not against it. You don't want to smash your hand into the bottle!

•➧ STEP THREE
Come to a rest. Successfully catching the bottle requires timing, and also balance. Practice balancing the bottle on the back of your hand if you have trouble making the bottle stall.

268 | POUR BEHIND THE HEAD

269 | POUR BEHIND THE BACK

•⇥ STEP ONE
Prepare a shaker or mixing glass on your work surface so it's ready to be added to (using whatever's in the bottle you're throwing).

•⇥ STEP TWO
Hold the bottle with your non-dominant hand so that the bottle is upright (called "forehand" in flair lingo).

•⇥ STEP THREE
Move hand and bottle behind your head and, with your dominant hand, grab it by the neck in a reverse grip, then shift into pouring position (called "backhand" in flair lingo).

•⇥ STEP FOUR
Pour into the shaker or mixing glass. Feeling like this is too easy for you? Try throwing the bottle when transferring it behind your head.

•⇥ STEP ONE
Prepare a shaker or mixing glass on your work surface so it's ready to be added to (using whatever's in the bottle you're throwing).

•⇥ STEP TWO
Pop the bottle up with three fingers, as in the Bottle Stall, so it moves toward the shoulder of your dominant hand.

•⇥ STEP THREE
Move hand and bottle behind your head and, with your dominant hand, grab it by the neck in a reverse grip, then shift into pouring position (called "backhand" in flair lingo).

•⇥ STEP FOUR
As soon as you let go of the bottle, turn your body toward your nondominant arm so that your hand moves behind your back to catch the bottle.

270 | SAY CHEERS . . . OR SLÁINTE! SALUD! PROST!

Now that you've got a drink in your hand and friends around the table, don't forget to wish each other well and toast the moment. The tradition of toasting can be traced back across many eras and continents—from the Mughal Empire in India to the Scandinavian Vikings (who, it's said, drank from the skulls of fallen foes). In ancient Greece, the practice of toasting was meant to guard against poisoning, as the clinking of glasses would ensure sharing each other's wine as it sloshed across the table. It's also said that the term for toasting came from the medieval practice of soaking spiced bread in mead. However it began, here are a few ways to mix up your usual refrain.

Chai yo!
GOOD LUCK!
Thailand

Na zdravi!
TO YOUR HEALTH
Czech Republic

Salud!
TO GOOD HEALTH!
Spain

Bunden i vejret eller resten i håret!
BOTTOMS UP, OR THE REST IN YOUR HAIR!
Denmark

Salud y amor y tiempo para disfrutarlo
HEALTH & LOVE & TIME TO ENJOY IT
A classic across many Spanish-speaking countries
Argentina

Stin eyiassou
TO YOUR HEALTH
Greece

Nazdarovya
TO YOUR HEALTH
Russia

Yum seng
TO AN EMPTY GLASS
China

L'chaim
TO LIFE
This Hebrew phrase will be recognizable to many
Israel

Here's mud in your eye!
The origin may be a reference to trench warfare, horse racing, Biblical faith-healing, or simply the sediment in the bottom of a drink
Great Britain

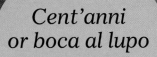
Cent'anni or boca al lupo
ONE HUNDRED YEARS OR AN EXPRESSION MEANING "GOOD LUCK"
Italy

Kampai or otsukare
"CHEERS" OR "YOU'RE TIRED"
COMPLIMENTS ONE'S WORK ETHIC—THEY DESERVE A DRINK!
Japan

Prost or Zum wohl
TO GOOD HEALTH
"PROST" FOR BEER, "ZUM WOHL" FOR WINE.
Germany

A votre sante
TO YOUR HEALTH
Respond with "a la votre" (and to yours)
France

Sláinte
GOOD HEALTH
Another option is from Jonathan Swift: "May you live all the days of your life."
Ireland

Stolyat
ONE HUNDRED YEARS
Poland

Oogy wawa!
CHEERS!
South Africa

271

BECOME A NEAT FREAK

Just as you can't be a great cook without tasting your ingredients, you can't improve at mixing drinks if you don't taste your spirits straight. When distillers make their products, they create them to taste great all by themselves. Yet most people have never tasted their favorite call liquor brand alone (moments of desperation aside).

Learning to taste and understand the flavors will allow you to develop your own recipes by finding complementary flavors. What's more, you may discover that some spirits are like peak-season tomatoes— they need little to nothing added.

272 { THROW NO STONES }

➤ If you enjoy drinking spirits neat, particularly whiskies, you'll eventually come across a gimmicky accessory in the form of cube-shaped rocks or hunks of metal designed to chill your spirit without diluting it. Well, save your money (spend the difference on a better bottle) since this is a solution without a problem. While a good number of brandies and whiskies are sold at 80 proof, many, in particular the special ones you would enjoy neat, are often sold at much higher proofs. You need and want the dilution that ice gives you. Even at standard strength—40 percent ABV, a potency that won't singe your palate—ice and dilution help aromatize many of the volatile essences in the spirit. Use one cube at a time, and when the contents of your glass get diluted and cold enough, simply remove the remaining ice with a spoon and enjoy.

273

TASTE LIKE A PRO

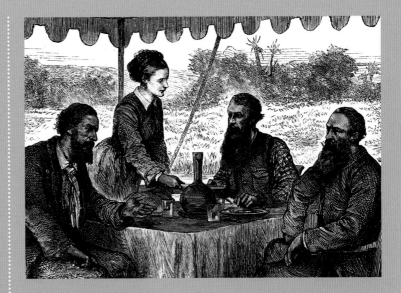

Once you've started tasting your spirits and getting used to trying them straight, you can experiment with the kind of set-up I use to taste spirits for reviews. At first, the hardest part will be identifying the specific aromas and flavors—your brain will tell you that it reminds you of something specific, but it won't say exactly what. It's a baffling feeling, much like seeing someone familiar but who you just can't place. Eventually, as you learn to pay attention, you'll start teasing out the specifics beyond the obvious like wood or alcohol—like particular fruits, spices, or even places. Here's how to begin.

FIND YOUR SPACE Possibly the most important—yet least obvious—factor in a fair tasting is finding a good place to do it—a place where you can conduct all your tastings. You'll need some space to spread out the bottles and glassware, and it's good to be aware of the kinds of smells in the room. One time I was perplexed by a bizarre floral smell everything had, until I finally realized it was the scent of fabric softener in the washing machine overwhelming my nose.

CHOOSE YOUR LIQUOR Try not to choose too many bottles at once, since the alcohol will dull your nose and palate quickly; 4 or 5 is a good target. Choosing a theme such as style or ingredients makes for a fun comparison.

VARY YOUR GLASSWARE The shape of the glasses you taste out of will affect the smells and often the taste of the spirit—the way prisms affect light, revealing different aspects. Get a collection of different shapes and pour the same spirit to see how different they seem. Choose at least two different shapes to taste out of.

DRINK IN ORDER Go from lightest and driest to sweetest and highest in alcohol.

HYDRATE LIBERALLY Needless to say, drink water in between tastes to cleanse your palate as much as possible.

SLOW DOWN TO SMELL Don't smell the spirit by jamming your nose in the glass like you would with wine—the higher proof may burn—and don't swirl the glass around, either. Give the glass a 45-degree tilt and move the glass slowly toward you to find the sweet spot where you can start to smell the different aromas. Then slowly move the glass around to see how they morph and change.

SIP TO TASTE Take a small sip and let it coat your tongue, then take a second sip and note the flavors, texture, strength, and sweetness. After you swallow, breathe in through your nose and then out through your mouth and you will get additional flavors that may have been overshadowed by the proof. Feel free to water things down if necessary, as hot tastings (both in proof and temperature) can be unpleasant.

274 GIVE A GOODY BAG

If you're hosting the kind of event you want your friends to talk about for years to come, you might consider a party favor for your guests to grab on their way home (provided they can still see straight). We're not talking engraved wedding favors or kiddie bags of candy, here, but something theme-appropriate or, ideally, drinkable.

Individual champagne splits (some even come in cans) tied with ribbon can do the trick, as can pre-bottled cocktails or fun-size nips from the liquor store. Tie a few together or push out the boat for the ones with the best (read: skull-shaped) packaging.

Maybe you served a signature cocktail or two at your shindig—print out the recipe and let your guests try their hand at home. Grab a handful of thematic accessories to toss in—like paper umbrellas or novelty cocktail swords.

Whip up a batch of rum balls if it's the holidays and pop a few into baggies, or serve individually packaged Jell-O shots (see item 239).

And if you'd rather send your guests home with aims at a better morning, get a megapack of water bottles and make them look extra festive for the taxi ride home.

275

GET INVITED BACK

If you're the guest—whether for a party or a weekend stay—remember to heed mom's advice and never arrive empty-handed. Sure, you can buy your host dinner or tote a bottle of wine, but if you want to ensure your place on the sleeper sofa, consider putting some thought into your offering. By this point, they've likely heard all about your cocktail-making talents, so here are a few host gifts that might prevent you from overstaying your welcome.

HOMEMADE ADDITIONS Whip up a tincture, infusion, or flavored syrup using your host's favorite flavors, or try something new and let your hosts join in on the cocktail experiments.

BARTENDING SERVICES Arrive bearing homemade ginger beer (see item 170), a bottle of vodka, and a bag of limes, and offer to set up shop for Moscow Mules (see item 169) all around.

TRAVEL COCKTAILS If they have upcoming travels scheduled (and who doesn't?), bring mini versions of their favorite cocktails—a nip of something, a garnish, and some fun novelty straws—to jazz up their free airplane soda.

BOOZY CANDY If all else fails, bring some boozy gummy bears or a box of liquor-packed sweets—from the store or homemade (see item 242).

276 | TACKLE THE CLEANUP

When it comes to cleanup, especially after a proper rager, you'll be sorely tempted to leave everything for the next day. That's what the day after the party is for, you'll think. And you're not wrong. But here's a tip: While you're still flush from your successful fete, walk around your place and collect all the stray glasses, bottles, and cans that have likely found their way into every corner. (Seriously: The bathroom always has at least one, and check behind the framed photos on your bookshelf, too.) Corral everything in the kitchen and—this is key—take out the recycling. Get the beer bottles and cans out of there, because there's nothing like that stale beer smell the next morning to make your hangover worse than it already is. Here are a few other ways to tackle the filthier parts of entertaining.

277 | GET OUT OF A STICK Y SITUATION

The biggest problem with spilling booze (aside from the waste of good booze) is that any residue left behind will get sticky. You'll need more than just a paper towel to rectify the situation, so turn to the old standbys: floor cleaners like Pine Sol or Simple Green, or simply dishwashing liquid mixed with water. You're going to need soap of one kind or another to avoid a squeaky reminder every time you walk by.

278

SAVE THE FURNITURE

Despite your extensive coaster collection (see item 045), you've discovered white rings on the heirloom coffee table, or there was a colossal spill all over the bar. Coat the mark with Vaseline, let it sit overnight, then wipe it away. Hopefully that's the worst of what you're dealing with postparty.

279 | GET SALTY

 Red wine spills are bound to happen, and there's a wealth of information online on how to save your carpet, couch, or designer suit. For how horrendous these spills appear at first glance, they can be surprisingly easy to clean up. First, let an old dishrag soak up as much as possible, then grab your salt shaker and generously coat the stain. Once it's dry, scrape and rinse (use club soda if needed) or blot with a sponge. Some people also swear by immediately rinsing a red wine spill with white wine. But why waste more wine?

280 | FINESSE YOUR FLASK

 A popular gift item and a surprisingly useful tool, the flask comes in enough varieties to suit everyone. But the dread of lingering flavors can keep some from ever making use of them. Here's how to get it properly clean (and properly rinsed) every time.

STEP ONE If this is a new flask, wash it with good ol' soap and water—just be careful about the amount of soap you use. You don't need much, and flasks can be notoriously tricky to rinse thoroughly. If you've already used too much soap, try rinsing with boiling water—and be sure to use a pot holder so you don't burn yourself.

STEP TWO If your flask requires a scrub, you'll be using some of the same tricks as you would on reusable water bottles. That means kosher salt, rice, Epsom salts, or baking soda, mixed with water (or white vinegar if you've got a particularly smelly vessel). Combine your scrubbing agent with your liquid and fill the flask about three-quarters of the way.

STEP THREE Cap it, and give it a good, lengthy shake. You want to be vigorous and not stop too soon. Pretend you're shaking James Bond's martini, and you better do it right. The salt or other agent will "scrub" the corners, and then you get to rinse the heck out of it.

STEP FOUR Rinse like crazy, and use boiling water if you're still finding salt in there.

281 { DEVISE A CURE }

American humorist Robert Benchley wrote, "The only cure for a real hangover is death." It might feel true, especially in the throes of your worst morning-afters, but there are a few other things you can try.

I wouldn't consider myself a model of restraint, nor a cautionary tale of excess, but I've had a hangover now and then, from bad influence, a miscalculation, or simply forgetting to eat. My own timeworn remedy is to sleep in, drink water until the idea of walking in public sounds reasonable, have a greasy breakfast (possibly with a brunch cocktail), and then get a large coffee to go. Even if eating doesn't sound appealing at the time, it will help. You will—slowly—start to feel normal, but you're in a triage situation, so don't get stuck in traps like juices or low-fat nonsense. This just isn't the time.

USBG | BOSTON CHAPTER

✦ FREDERIC YARM ✦

Lead Bartender | Loyal Nine

282 ✕ GET A COLA CLEAR-OUT

At one of Yarm's jobs, the hangover cure of choice was soda-gun Pepsi with 10 dashes of Angostura bitters—to help down two Advils from the first-aid kit. The Pepsi delivered sugar, water, electrolytes, and a bit of caffeine, and the Angostura was a godsend, with a bounty of botanicals to settle the stomach. Finally, the Advil and caffeine helped clear the cobwebs.

283

GO PRO

Take it from the pros—they know what they're talking about. Alexandra F. Williams, the USBG membership coordinator, recommends Condition, a Korean herbal concoction available at some Asian markets for around five bucks a pop. "This magical mix of ancient medicine is the best thing to happen to heavy drinking since the Old Fashioned."

Ralf Ramirez of the Los Angeles chapter mixes bitters and soda for his remedy—fill a tall glass with ice, add 4–6 dashes of your favorite bitters, and top with seltzer water. Garnish with a lime or lemon wedge and you'll have a refreshing concoction that looks more elegant than you do.

284 ❖ BITE THE DOG BACK

"A little hair of the dog that bit ya"— this fabled hangover cure dates back to medieval times, when the (suspicious at best) cure for what ailed you was more of what ailed you.
The belief was that if you were bitten by a rabid dog, you needed to burn some of the dog's hair and place it over the bite. Shockingly, this "cure" for rabies didn't work. But the myth—as it relates to alcohol—persists (though actress Tallulah Bankhead once said, "It's as logical as trying to put out a fire with applications of kerosene"). Give it a whirl and enjoy a brunch cocktail, by all means. But if you're bitten by a dog, best consult a doctor.

✦ COREY CREASON ✦

Bartender

285

EAT AND ENERGIZE

This particular cure is for those days when the hangover is crushing your soul but you still have to get up and conquer the world. Drink 1 liter of coconut water and a 12-oz energy drink—Red Bull is a go-to when coffee simply won't cut it. Then eat two egg white sandwiches with sausage, on rolls, smothered in ketchup and hot sauce (Cholula recommended).

In Closing

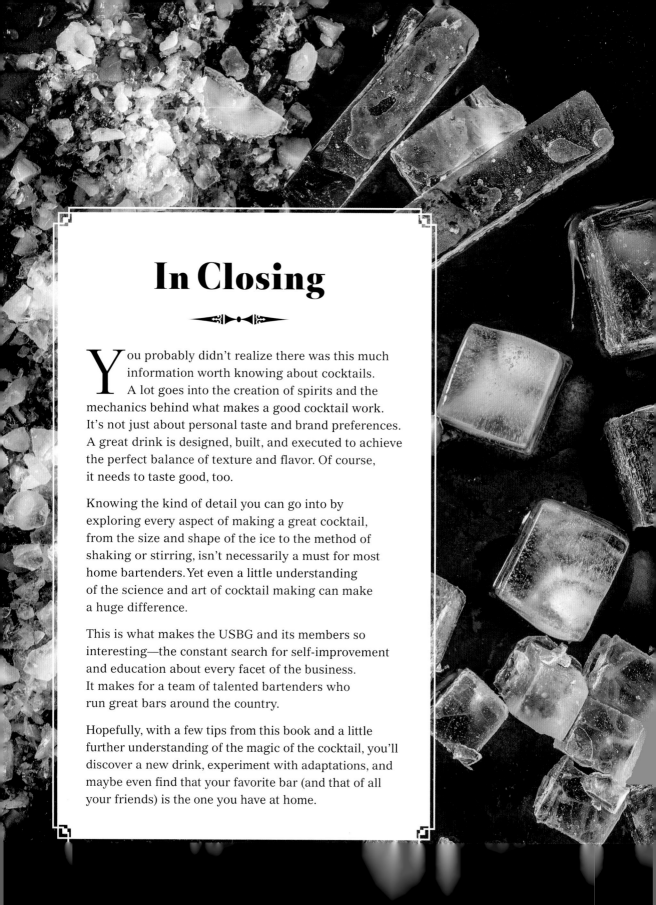

You probably didn't realize there was this much information worth knowing about cocktails. A lot goes into the creation of spirits and the mechanics behind what makes a good cocktail work. It's not just about personal taste and brand preferences. A great drink is designed, built, and executed to achieve the perfect balance of texture and flavor. Of course, it needs to taste good, too.

Knowing the kind of detail you can go into by exploring every aspect of making a great cocktail, from the size and shape of the ice to the method of shaking or stirring, isn't necessarily a must for most home bartenders. Yet even a little understanding of the science and art of cocktail making can make a huge difference.

This is what makes the USBG and its members so interesting—the constant search for self-improvement and education about every facet of the business. It makes for a team of talented bartenders who run great bars around the country.

Hopefully, with a few tips from this book and a little further understanding of the magic of the cocktail, you'll discover a new drink, experiment with adaptations, and maybe even find that your favorite bar (and that of all your friends) is the one you have at home.

INDEX

ACKNOWLEDGMENTS

I'd like to thank my liver for its tireless optimism, help and support. I couldn't have done it without you. I am grateful to Bee for her belief and encouragement when mine waned, along with her recipe testing skills that made it especially fun when it could have simply been more work. Thanks to everyone at Weldon Owen for making the book a reality and visually appealing and grammatically correct, in particular Bridget Fitzgerald, Marisa Kwek, Jennifer Durant, Mariah Bear, and Ian Cannon. The title couldn't have happened without the cooperation of all the members of the USBG who took time out of their busy schedules to share their knowledge, recipes, and skills. Also at the USBG, I need to recognize Alexandra Williams, Aaron Gregory Smith, and David Nepove for facilitating the connection to the thousands of members. Photographers John Lee and Valter Fabiano were amazing, making the book come to life. Finally, I'd like to thank Lance Winters for letting me steal some of his jokes.

ABOUT THE AUTHOR

Growing up, Lou Bustamante wanted to be a "mad scientist," working in a lab filled with alchemical devices, bubbling beakers, and tesla coils. Naturally, this led him into the liquor business, where concocting magical tonics and distillates using arcane machines is standard.

A spirits professional who has filled a considerable number of roles within the industry, Lou has done everything from working at a distillery, bartending, teaching cocktail classes, designing whiskey labels, to developing recipes and products and importing 20 tons of whole cooked agave pinas from Tequila, Mexico.

He has also served on the San Francisco Chapter's elected council of the USBG as Secretary and Treasurer, and been an active member for many years.

He has written about bars, restaurants, and spirits for *Wine & Spirits Magazine, The San Francisco Chronicle, Tasting Table, Thrillist,* and *SF Weekly,* among others.

On average, he tastes some 500 cocktails a year, and has only occasionally ended up hungover.

CREDITS

PHOTOGRAPHS COURTESY OF THE FOLLOWING:
Kelly Booth: 148, 149; Lou Bustamante: 033, 064, 143, 152, 181, 226, 245; Alice Gao: 243, 244; iStock: 093, 222, 262, 276; Nader Khouri: TOC (Entertaining & Hospitality), ch 1 opener spread, 040, 054, 121, 218, 222, rimmed glasses spread, ch 3 closing spread; Erin Kunkel: 030; John Lee: cover, title, title half, 005, 032, 035, 036, 038, 043, 044, 045, 077, 079, 116, 118, 119, 125, 141, 251, 253, 257, closing half, back credits; Robyn Lehr: 228; Cindy Loughridge: 215, 217; Eric Piasecki/OTTO: 216; Shutterstock: content half, 002, 006, 008, 009, 010, 013, 015, 017, 019, 020, 027, 028, 029, 051, 052, 053, 069, 082, 083, 084, 085, 096, 097, 103, 105, 113, 114, 115, 158, 160, 161, 172, 180, 184, 189, 190, 192, 199, 200, 201, ch3 opener spread, 211, 212, 214, 239, 259, 261, 270, 271, 273; Valter Fabiano: About the USBG, The Cocktail Has Changed, 024, 042, 227, 249, Recipes & Techniques intro, 055, 063, 075, 076, 091, 111, bartop spread, 117, 119, 133, 134, 168, 169, 188, 193, 205, 207, 208, 227, 249, back cover; Stocksy: content half, candle spread, ch2 opener spread, 126, 162, 164, 165, 175, 182, 223, 231, 233, 238, 274, 275, 285; Allison Webber: Basics & Setup intro

ILLUSTRATIONS COURTESY OF THE FOLLOWING:
Tim McDonagh: 007, 025, 031, 034 (bottom row), 039, 052, 070, 072, 099 108, 114, 122, 129, 132, 137, 145, 147, 150, 151, 154, 174, 177, 195, 200, 210, 221, 230, 240, 260, 263, 284; Klaus Meinhardt: 034 (top row), 035, 047, 065, 117, 120, 167, 170, 229, 247, 256, 257, 264,

267-269; Shutterstock (icons): 001, 003, 008, 010, 011, 012, 014, 019, 020, 024, 026, 031, 036, 039, 041, 046, 048, 049, 050, 053, 056, 061, 063, 064, 066, 067, 069, 071, 072, 075, 081, 084, 085, 086, 088, 090, 091, 092, 094, 097, 098, 101, 102, 103, 104, 105, 106, 108, 111, 112, 115, 116, 122, 123, 124, 126, 127, 130, 133, 134, 135, 136, 139, 140, 142, 143, 144, 146, 149, 151, 152, 155, 158, 159, 161, 165, 168, 169, 172, 173, 176, 179, 180, 181, 183,184, 185, 186, 187, 190, 191, 192, 194, 196, 197, 198, 201, 204, 205, 206, 208, 209, 212, 215, 218, 225, 232, 235, 236, 237, 238, 250, 252, 258, 272, 273, 279, 280; Shutterstock (surface backgrounds): 012, 025, 059, 060, 126, 154, 171, 176, 178, 179, 183, 232, 239, 266, 270

EQUIPMENT COURTES OF THE FOLLOWING:
Cocktail Kingdom (barspoons): 005, 042, 077, 078; Kegworks; Mr. Mojito (mojito muddlers): 005, 042, 044; Tommy's Margarita Mix: 152; Umami Mart; Urban Bar: 005 (double-sided jigger, Hawthorne strainer), 042 (double-sided jigger), 044 (Cobbler shaker, double-sided jigger, garnish tongs, ice bucket), 077 (mixing glasses), 116 (Boston shaker, Calabrese Parisian shaker, Cobbler shaker, 118 (Hawthorne strainer, Julep strainer)

SPECIAL THANKS TO THE FOLLOWING LOCATIONS:
15 Romolo, La Mar, Comstock Saloon, the Armory, Pagan Idol

weldon**owen**

PRESIDENT & PUBLISHER	Roger Shaw
SVP, SALES & MARKETING	Amy Kaneko
FINANCE & OPERATIONS DIRECTOR	Philip Paulick
ASSOCIATE PUBLISHER	Mariah Bear
EDITOR	Bridget Fitzgerald
CREATIVE DIRECTOR	Kelly Booth
ART DIRECTOR	Marisa Kwek
SENIOR PRODUCTION DESIGNER	Rachel Lopez Metzger
DESIGNER	Jennifer Durrant
PRODUCTION DIRECTOR	Chris Hemesath
ASSOCIATE PRODUCTION DIRECTOR	Michelle Duggan
IMAGING MANAGER	Don Hill

Weldon Owen would like to thank Marisa Solis for her editorial services, and Kevin Broccoli for the index.

EXECUTIVE DIRECTOR	Aaron G. Smith
NATIONAL PRESIDENT	David Nepove
NATIONAL VICE PRESIDENT	Kyle McHugh
NATIONAL TREASURER	Laura Cullen
NATIONAL SECRETARY	Nicola Riske

Library of congress cataloging in publication data is available.

ISBN-13 9781681880990
ISBN-10: 1-68188-099-7

10 9 8 7 6 5 4 3 2 1
2016 2017 2018 2019

Printed in China by 1010